TEN *of the* LARGEST

CHURCH
MINISTRIES

AGGRESSIVELY
TOUCHING THE WORLD

TEN *of the* LARGEST

CHURCH MINISTRIES

AGGRESSIVELY
TOUCHING THE WORLD

ELMER L. TOWNS

DESTINY IMAGE® PUBLISHERS, INC.
P.O. Box 310, Shippensburg, PA 17257-0310
"Promoting Inspired Lives."

This book and all other Destiny Image and Destiny Image Fiction books are available at Christian bookstores and distributors worldwide.

Cover design by: Eileen Rockwell

For more information on foreign distributors, call 717-532-3040.

Reach us on the Internet: www.destinyimage.com.

ISBN 13 TP: 978-0-7684-5466-6

ISBN 13 eBook: 978-0-7684-5467-3

ISBN 13 HC: 978-0-7684-5469-7

ISBN 13 LP: 978-0-7684-5468-0

For Worldwide Distribution, Printed in the U.S.A.

1 2 3 4 5 6 7 8 / 24 23 22 21 20

CONTENTS

SECTION ONE

The Church of the Highlands, Birmingham, Alabama—55,000 worshipers. The faith of Chris Hodges planted The Church of the Highlands, a multi-site church of almost 40 locations in Alabama. He also began Highlands College training leaders for ministry, plus he has a coaching network of over 17,000 churches.

Hillsong Church, Australia—150,000 worshipers. The faith of Brian Houston built the largest Christian ministry that influences the world through church planting, television and social media. Houston also found Hillsong Music, Hillsong International Leadership College, which is located in several nations around the world with students representing 70 countries, and Hillsong TV Channel is seen in over 180 countries.

Life.Church, Oklahoma City—100,000 worshipers. The faith of Craig Groeschel built Life.Church into the largest attended church in the U.S. with over 40 campuses across America and influencing millions through social media and television. Pastor Groeschel planted the church in a two-car garage in Oklahoma City in 1991, and has produced the YouVersion of the Bible with over 375 million downloaded apps.

World Harvest Center, Fiji—vision to plant 100,000 churches. Pastor Suliasi Kurulo, a government engineer, began knocking on every door on his island to lead people to Jesus, and then planted a church to finish the task. Next, he planned to knock on every door on every island in Fiji and planted over 300 churches to complete the task. Now he has planted over 7,000 churches throughout the Pacific Rim, and has a vision of planting 100,000 churches.

The Redeemed Christian Church of God, Nigeria planted 42,000 churches. The faith of Enoch Adeboye, Overseer and pastor of The Redeemed Christian Church of God, planted over 40,000 churches in 180 nations around the world. Enoch Adeboye has a Ph.D in mathematics and is a former university lecturer with a vision of planting a church within five minutes of everyone in major locations around the world. The first Holy Ghost Congress was held in 1998, with over seven million attendees, the largest gathering of people according to CNN and BBC.

Global Church Network—attempting to complete the Great Commission by 2030 A.D. The faith of James O. Davis, founder and president, synergizes world influencing mega churches as well as church planting agencies with conferences around the world to share strategy, vision and news, plus instructs over 60,000 church planters with online training, and face to face teaching in over 100 HUBS around the world.

Glory of Zion, Corinth, Texas—60,000 worshipers. The faith of Chuck Pierce built one of the largest churches on the internet by live streaming church worship services worldwide to aligned believers. This church also includes a network of house churches, regular churches and Christian businesses.

New Life Assembly of God, Chennai, India—60,000 worshipers. The New Life Assembly of God, Chennai, South India (previously known as Madras), is the largest attended church in India (fourth largest city, population 8 million) with an average of 50,000 worshipers weekly in 5 campuses, and has planted 150 churches, and sends out missionaries around the world. Rev. David Mohan began with 7 people in 1973, and today is called by evangelicals the spiritual father of India.

Word of Hope Church, Manila, Philippines—60,000 worshipers. David Sobrepeña, founder and pastor, was a financial money manager who left his job in America to return to Manila, Philippines to plant a church that today has over 60,000 in attendance, with 60 satellite churches. In addition, he has planted over 300 independent churches in the Philippines, and a Bible college and other extensive ministries. His vision is to pastor 100,000 worshipers.

Love Fellowship, Southern Asia—Translating Scriptures to plant churches to evangelize unreached people groups. The faith of Dr. Raj to plant 40,000 house churches and 5,000 street churches in every unreached people group in his South Asian nation, by translating Scriptures into all its languages. Raj sends church planters to unreached villages as "the man of peace" to share the gospel by gathering a team to translate the Bible from a trade language (Hindi) into a minority language using Church Centric Bible Translation philosophy (CCBT).

SECTION TWO

Faith's Crucible: God allows leaders to go through the crucible of testing to empty themselves of self and pride and be filled with God's anointing to purify their faith to accomplish what God has called them to do.

Crucible Faith is learned in the crisis of a dark midnight experience when the leader is shut up to God only, and surrenders sin and selfishness to totally depend on God and find His direction, and discover His power to work through them.

Brinkmanship Faith Principle: In a time of crisis, a leader must turn aside from dangers to act on their faith, work wisely and diligently to solve the immediate problems/crises.

In a time of crisis, God will use a leader to act on faith to solve a problem by applying faith-answers to the crisis.

Reciprocity of Faith and Vision: A vision from God challenges leaders to launch out in faith to begin ministry and their faith grows stronger as the leader accomplishes the vision.

Faith involves seeing a need, and determining a plan how God wants that need to be met, and as the plan becomes a reality, both faith and vision grow.

Objectifying Faith Principle (Say-It Faith): The first step of leaders in completing a project is speaking or objectifying what needs to be done, knowing God is leading to accomplish the task, and when leaders and followers understand and apply faith in God, they will begin solving the challenges at hand.

> Leaders must speak or objectify to follow the plan God wants done, then work with followers to accomplish the task or solve the problem.

15 Transferable Faith

Transferable Faith: Growing leaders can find and develop faith when they identify with the model of a strong faith-driven leader who as their example, guides their growth in faith.

> The expression of faith found in great leaders can be communicated to aspiring leaders by example.

16 Second-Generation Faith

Second-Generation Faith: Is a commitment to the same values and vision as the first-generational faith, then fighting the same battles; and adapting their faith to changing culture and new emerging issues.

> Second-generation faith is committed to the same values and vision of the first generation, and will face the same battles; but stands on the shoulders of the first generation to reach higher (vision), do more, and do it better in a new culture and for a new generation.

17 The Gift of Faith

Gift of Faith Principle: Is the ability of the leader trusting God to divinely intervene in an issue or crisis that is facing a ministry, so the work of God goes forward.

True faith is the most active motivating power in the whole world. "Faith, which worketh by love," works all sorts of marvels; and where there is this true faith, it will prove its reality by its practicableness. —Charles Spurgeon

SECTION THREE

MEETING EXTRAORDINARY LEADERS,

Encountering Great Church Ministries

This book is not just about ten big church ministries, because their large size is not the only reason I write. It is about their current growth, as seen in their energy and potential. But most of all, it is about their influence on other church ministries around the world. This book is about world evangelism and aggressively completing the Great Commission.

This book will emphasize four areas. Why they were chosen? First, the leader's faith; second, the impact of their worldwide influences; third, the method or ministry they used to influence the world; and fourth, their aggressive dedication to complete the Great Commission.

LESSONS ON FAITH

First, you will read something about the faith of each leader who is the human driving force behind each church ministry. Jesus challenged, "Have faith in God" (Mark 11:22). But this was more than salvation faith and more than living by faith. Jesus instructed that when "God's faith" was working, then it was possible to "say to the mountain (barrier), move...it will move" (Mark 11:23, ELT). So this book will analyze each leader's expression of faith that moved mountains to build their ministry.

Many of the lessons of faith I've learned from these leaders are included in the pages of this book. So, read this book—not because of who I am—but because of the lessons you'll learn from leaders as they express their great faith.

Every time I learned great insight from any pastor, I used that understanding to probe next time I wrote about another great leader. Just as great leaders influence their followers to great works, so the greatness of the faith of the leaders in this book motivated me to find out more about faith. Now, I want you to learn faith from them. (See Chapter 15, "Transferable Faith.")

This book ties together many facets of faith. Basically, each leader expresses their experiences of faith that characterize their walk with God resulting in their aggressive ministry. The faith experience in each was in some ways a different expression of faith from other great leaders.

The difference in spiritual giftedness among great leaders motivated them to minister their faith differently. Some built great churches on their great preaching ability. Sometimes it was their ability to raise money; other times it was their ability to organize and manage. Other times it was their ability to serve and be constantly in the homes, hospitals, and places of business where their people were hurting and needed them. God uses different leaders with different expressions of faith to accomplish His work through different personalities, cultures, and races (the basic thesis of this book).

LESSONS OF INFLUENCE

Second, you will read the various areas of influence by these church ministries. Some influence by church planting, others by television, others by education, and still others by translating Scriptures into the language of an unreached people group that led to church planting. Note carefully how the influences of these church ministries are still growing and being used of God.

There are many megachurch/ministries/denominations in Nigeria, Africa, but only The Redeemed Christian Church of God was chosen to be included in this book because of its purpose and worldwide influence. The same could be said of several large Christian radio and television ministries, but Hillsong is doing it many ways and doing it effectively. I was not just looking for big church ministries, I was looking for the most current aggressive ministries.

LESSONS OF METHODS

Third, I was looking for the method used by church ministries to make them influential. The question was asked, "What methods is a church ministry using that makes it effective?" When looking at methods used by Christians in ministry, specifically church ministries, remember: "Methods are a human application to reach people for Christ; they are an extension of God's eternal principles." These eternal principles found in Scriptures never change, but they are applied differently in each generation and differently in each culture to reach people with the gospel and win them to salvation.

> Methods are many,
> Principles are few,
> Methods may change,
> But principles never do.

In 1969, I wrote an extremely popular book that stayed on the list of bestselling books for fourteen months—*The 10 Largest Sunday Schools and What Made Them Grow. Christian Bookseller's Magazine* quoted, "It was a *thunderbolt* across the Christian church." C. Peter Wagner, church growth professor at Fuller Theological Seminary said, "This book introduced the Christian world to the megachurch movement and paved the way for the growth of large churches in the 1970s."

This present book, *Ten of the Largest Church Ministries Aggressively Touching the World,* can have the same influence. My previous book introduced church leadership to using Sunday school evangelism as the basis for building large churches. Sunday school buses was the method used by large churches for outreach.

However, those church growth methods of the '70s won't work in the 2020s. It will take new workable evangelistic growth methods. The ten church ministries in this book are returning to the original mandate of Jesus Christ, which is church planting. Reaching the world can't be done by just radio or television alone, nor can it be done by personal evangelism alone, or gospel preaching alone. To reach the world for Jesus Christ we must plant churches in every culture where new converts are baptized, taught the Word of God, trained in godly living, and equipped for evangelistic outreach. Then that church sets out to reproduce another church.

LESSON OF AGGRESSION

These ten leaders are ministering aggressively with time restraints to complete the Great Commission in their ministry. They are using every available method to reach every available person at every available time to finish in their lifetime. James Davis of Global Church Network (Chapter 6) has targeted A.D. 2030 (2,000 years since Pentecost) because when the last unreached people group is reached, then Jesus will return to take His church to heaven to be with them (see 1 Thess. 4:13-18).

LEARN FROM LEADERS

These ten large church ministries are telling well the old story of Jesus' death for all. They are involving many in the task of using unique church planting evangelistic methods to reach the world for Jesus Christ.

Look at the various ways they plant churches; look at the various ways they teach and disciple their people to live for Christ. Look at the various ways they reach and win people to Jesus. Look at all they do and learn from their church. Learn from their leaders. Learn what the Holy Spirit is teaching in your thoughts and dreams.

While writing this book, I talked to Dan Manley, a Lynchburg pastor who was a high school student who ministered with Jerry Falwell, pastor of Thomas Road Baptist Church, to lead people to Christ. In the 1960s they visited a couple—the wife had come forward the previous Sunday to be saved. Her husband was an alcoholic.

Manley tells of finding four empty beer bottles on the kitchen table. Jerry never said a word about drinking or giving up drinking. He talked about Jesus and following Jesus.

"I can't come to church," the husband said, "I don't have a shirt or shoes." Danny thought, *How would Jesus answer the man?*

Quickly Jerry stood up, removed his coat, took off his shirt and tie, and gave them to the man. Then he handed the man his shoes and socks. Jerry Falwell went home barefooted and without his shirt. There he got completely dressed so he could continue his visitation in the neighborhood.

The husband came forward the next Sunday morning to receive Jesus Christ and became a faithful Sunday school teacher at Thomas Road Baptist Church. That's sacrificial faith...the absolute necessity to build a world-influencing ministry.

TEN METHODS TO EXAMINE

As you read this book, think about the following ten methods or activities you see in these ten churches. Could you learn their biblical potential? Could you adapt them to your ministry and could they be used effectively in your ministry?

1. The Church of the Highlands: the mechanics of ministry

2. Hillsong: the power of worship

3. Life.Church: apply marketing techniques to evangelism

4. World Harvest Center: the power of personal evangelism—knocking on doors

5. The Redeemed Christian Church of God: power of vision

6. Global Church Network: the power of a goal to aggressively complete the Great Commission

7. Glory of Zion: building an internet church of 60,000

8. New Life Assembly of God: turning a mission field into a mission force

9. Word of Hope: power of sacrificing all

10. Dr. Raj: South Asia—evangelism by Scripture translation

SEVEN QUESTIONS TO HELP GUIDE YOUR READING

As you read these ten life stories of extraordinary faith, try to find answers to the following seven questions designed to help you think about and analyze how a church or ministry can influence the world for God. These seven questions have grown out of a study of faith, and each of the seven questions are systematically answered in chapters 11-16.

Chapter 11: *Faith's Crucible*: How was the faith of each leader tested and deepened?

Chapter 12: *Brinkmanship Faith*: What crisis did the leader face, and how did his faith help solve the problem?

Chapter 13: *Reciprocity of Faith and Vision*: How did the leader's faith and vision interact to build his ministry?

Chapter 14: *Objectifying Faith:* How did the leader's expression of faith influence the growth of his ministry and what about the ministry was prospered?

Chapter 15: *Transferable Faith:* Who influenced the faith of the leader to build a world-influencing ministry and seven experience of faith was transferred?

Chapter 16: *Second-Generation Faith:* What is the faith expression of the second-generation, and what strengths do they retain and what changes were made for continued growth?

Chapter 17: *The Gift of Faith:* Does God give more faith for ministry to some than to others? Yet using the faith you have is the basis for having more faith.

I've written this book not to impress you with the greatest of faith in men and women of God. Also, I've not written this book to impress you with my understanding of all the principles it takes to activate faith. No, I've written this book to activate your faith. Faith is as simple as loving. You can meet someone and love them simply by expressing love. You can meet God and have faith in Him simply by expressing your faith to Him. Faith is simply your relationship with God; it's as simple as knowing God and letting God know you. But just as love can grow to an immense depth over the years when you live together with someone you love...so faith can grow to the same intensity based on your continued, unending, growing relationship with God over the years.

Because of this book, may you reach out in faith to touch God—and may God reach out to move your mountain.

Sincerely yours,

Elmer Towns

TEN OF THE LARGEST CHURCH MINISTRIES

Aggressively Influencing World Evangelism

Chapter 1

FAITH TO BUILD A MULTI-SITE CHURCH

with More Than 55,000 Worshipers

Church of the Highlands
Birmingham, Alabama
Chris Hodges, Pastor

Chris Hodges, founder and pastor, Church of the Highlands, Birmingham, Alabama, leads 54 worship services at 22 campuses and 19 of Alabama's correctional facilities, with more than 55,000 worshipers each weekend. He also founded Highlands College to train ministry leaders and helps resource over 11,000 churches with the same goals in ministry.

What kind of faith does a leader need to plant and build one of the most attended churches in America? What shapes and influences his faith? How did he express his faith to plan a strategy to keep growing the Church of the Highlands? How does Hodges serve so many people?

A VISIT WILL EXPLAIN WHY

When I drove into the four-lane parkway leading up to the Church of the Highlands (high on the top of a hill), there were workers everywhere. Dozens of parking attendants directing traffic or driving visitors to the auditorium. I was met by greeters who told me their name...asked me my name and directed me to the hospitality tables to register. There were dozens of ushers who were hovering to make everyone comfortable. Back stage there were people getting everything ready. I thought to myself, "Chris Hodges must be an organizational genius to recruit and motivate hundreds of volunteers serving early Wednesday morning." Everywhere I went, workers were swarming.

The platform and staff were filled with youthful people (to me, I am 87 years old). There was energy...excitement...and expectancy. Hodges says, "Youth want to be recruited and put to work in ministry."

I've interviewed many of the pastors of the largest churches in the U.S. and around the world; they usually explain the *dynamics* of growth...and numbers...and programs. Not Chris Hodges; he spent the first hour explaining the spiritual nature of the *mechanics* of growth.

Where do we begin to understand the growth and power of a church of 55,000 worshipers? Hodges says, "Our system delivers the message and results." Then he explained from the platform, "The system is the *how* of ministry that determines the *what* of ministry that accomplishes the *vision* of ministry."

He pointed out the success of McDonald's hamburgers. "The product (a hamburger), doesn't make McDonald's one of the most profitable fast food chains in the world. The system of McDonald's (fast, economical, clean, courteous) determines its success."

"We have the greatest gospel to offer to people, but most churches don't know how to deliver it to the public."

"Many small churches have a delivery system that is designed to get small results. They hang on to their small delivery system and stay small." So Hodges constantly asks himself how his church can do it better. "I want a system that puts my vision to work...effectively."

Hodges told an audience, "If no one is getting saved, and no one is being delivered, and no one is volunteering to work in ministry, then you are doing it wrong." He asked three questions:

First, *"What are you counting*? If nickels and noses is where you focus your ministry, then that is the wrong focus. You should be counting how many people are in ministry, how many people are getting discipled."

Second, *"What do you communicate*? You don't communicate to your people what you do; you communicate who you are!"

Third, *"What do you celebrate*?" He wants to create a worship service that lost people love to attend. Hodges wants people to enjoy church, look forward to attending, and feel they have missed something important if they miss it.

SMALL GROUPS

The church has approximately 55,000 people in small groups. Hodges tells everyone, "Create small groups where people experience community, find freedom, and grow every way, but primarily spiritually." It is in these small groups people find transformation and then experience transformation.

In life, everyone is already in small groups. So create small groups to get them into a small group in the church. How important are small groups? In Hodges' thinking—"Imperative!"

"Church of the Highlands is small groups." Then Hodges explains, "We are not a church that just has small groups."

Hodges explained four principles that guide their groups:

First, total commitment to small groups. If you don't have people relating to one another, then your church is only a crowd.

Second, allow people to form groups based on their interests.

Third, intentionally form "need groups," i.e., men, women, students, marriage, outreach, service, prayer, etc.

Fourth, use events to promote groups. Hodges says, "We are not an event church that has small groups, we are a small group church that has events."

SPIRITUAL GIFTS

Because this is a church with a Pentecostal heritage, people immediately think of sign gifts. But that is not Hodges' first emphasis. "Create a process where people can find their spiritual gifts." By that he means giftedness to serve and worship God. Then he adds, "Don't recruit for service in ministry; help people discover their spiritual gift for ministry." To do this Hodges would ask everyone, "What has God designed you to be in life and do in life?"

How does Hodges help them discover God's design for their life?

1. Explain the vison of the church and give everyone an opportunity to become a member—a part of the ministry.

2. Help them discover their God-given design for their life (personality profiles and spiritual gift profiles). When people discover God's design for their life, they find what or how they are supposed to serve.

3. Teach leadership and prepare them to serve in ministry and on a Dream Team.

4. Help them join a team. Hodges says, "We don't talk them into service, we get them to say 'I was made for this.'"

The secret of thousands of workers: "I don't start ministries; I empower leaders to do ministry." How does Hodges do this? "I create a procedure where every person can serve on a team connected to their dream."

Then to add an explanation, Hodges says, "You can't create a culture in a church, you must be the culture. You can't create worshipers, you must worship. Don't emphasize what you want people to do; you must be what you want them to be, and you must do what you want them to do. Excellence is an absolute necessity. Excellence creates culture."

"Don't tell people what they need to do; help them find out what God has designed them to do."

MAKING OF A LEADER

Chris Hodges began attending church literally in the nursery, the Sunday after he was born. His mom and dad were devoted Southern Baptists in Baton Rouge, Louisiana, where his dad played the organ in church for 30 years. At the age of seven, Chris walked the aisle and was baptized but shares that he did not have a conversion experience until he was 15 years old. At that age he ran across a verse that shook him: "Not everyone who says to me, 'Lord, Lord,' will enter the kingdom of heaven, but only the one who does the will of my Father who is in heaven" (Matt. 7:21 NIV). Chris then realized obtaining eternal life had nothing to do with religion but everything to do with a personal relationship with Jesus.

As a result of his experience, Chris finds great joy in ministering to people so that they too can know God in an intimate relationship with Jesus as their Savior. This emphasis may be one of the key ingredients that makes Church of the Highlands so successful. Chris said, "When I was praying about planting this church, I asked God to put it where there were many lost people who were members of churches but did not know God."

So in his altar call he will often say, "If you consider yourself a Christian but you don't know God personally, you can meet Jesus Christ right now and be born again." He estimates tens of thousands of people are saved every year through that invitation in the Deep South, where going to church and being a believer can be more cultural than personal.

"I was an accounting major at Louisiana State University, following the tradition of my father who had been a legislative auditor for the State of Louisiana," Chris said. "Between my sophomore and junior years, I served in a Christian summer camp and took a missions trip. I totally fell in love with ministry and transferred to Gulf States Bible College in Baton Rouge. A church hired me as a youth minister while I was still a student, and then I transitioned to Colorado Springs, Colorado, to minister in another church. I served there for seven years then returned to my home church in Baton Rouge to serve as an associate pastor for another seven years."

God then led Chris to make a leap of faith. "During this season of my life, I was committed to 21 days of prayer and fasting. On the 17th day, I had an open vision of me preaching in a building, located on an interstate, in a Southern city. I did not know the city. After talking to my pastor about my vision, I decided to do something about it, so I took my family on vacation in search of that city.

"When I entered Birmingham, Alabama, I did not know a single person in town, but God gave me a supernatural love for that city. That is the only way I can describe God leading me to Birmingham. I remember being on a high point overlooking a six-lane highway during a huge traffic jam when the Spirit of God spoke to my heart: 'You are going to pastor the people in that traffic jam.' So I obeyed and moved to Birmingham."

SPIRITUAL FOUNDATION

When asked about the incredible growth of Church of the Highlands, Chris said, "If there is any secret to our church's growth, it is our commitment to 21 days of prayer and fasting—twice every year in January and August. January because it is the beginning of the calendar year, and I want our people to be spiritually ready for the coming new year. August because it is the beginning of the school year; summer is over and the fall requires new energy. I want that energy for our church outreaches. It is powerful to see over 11,000 people showing up to pray at 6:00 in the morning."

Hodges says these 21 days are "intentional" for both church and people. People begin a new year in God's presence, and they begin the fall challenge of school and new business initiatives by focusing on attaining goals. Why shouldn't the church do the same?

IMPARTING VISION

Hodges said before their first Sunday meeting in 2001, they had a practice service with a small team of about 50 people who were going to help launch the church. He didn't know why he did this, but he brought them all up on the stage. He told them the story of Abraham and how God took Abraham outside and said, "Look up... see the stars, you shall have that many offspring." Then Hodges told his team to turn around to look at the empty seats. It was a 1,000-seat fine arts theater in Mountain Brook High School. He asked them, "What do you all see?" And at that moment of time everyone on the team started weeping. They could see in their minds and hearts an auditorium filled with people. He told them, "When this building is completely full, I am going to bring you all back on stage to let you actually see what you saw in the Spirit."

Eight months later when they had 1,000 people that Sunday, the church did not know why he invited the original launch team up on the stage with him. It was to let them actually see what they saw in their hearts and spirits eight months earlier. The key for leaders is to see it before anyone else does. The greatest commodity of leaders is communicating the vision God gives them.

"I use vision to help our people see God's future for our church. The best kind of faith is the kind that sees what God sees. The Bible calls it, 'the substance of things hoped for...the evidence of things not seen' (Heb. 11:1). You see things physically in front of you, but you do not have evidence of what they mean. But if you can see them in your spirit, you have a picture in your heart. Faith is the ability to see what God is showing you. Faith happens whenever a revelation happens, whenever you read the Scripture and suddenly it becomes *Rhema*, God revealing His Word to you. You can see it outside of natural eyes, viewing it in your spirit, and that is what builds your faith. These experiences produce hope."

INFLUENCING OTHER CHURCHES

Hodges said, "I believe God ultimately wants to use our church not only to reach our state but to build something that is reproducible for other states and around the world. When we have anything programmatic, we ask, 'Could other churches do this?' I believe Church of the Highlands is called to be a model that other churches can follow as God leads them. Right now, we are providing resources for more than 11,000 churches in America into the system God originally showed me. That system is called *Grow*. I want them to take people on a clear spiritual journey not only to attract the lost but also to see them saved and assimilated into the body and get them serving in the church."

The church simulcasts the sermon portion of the worship service from the Grant Mills campus to its other campuses via a video feed. Each campus has its own pastor, worship experience, and small group gatherings. Each campus has various ministry opportunities and teams for those who attend branch campuses to minister through their location. Each campus also has its own weekly prayer gathering.

Hodges says, "I was one of the six leaders who helped start ARC (Association of Related Churches). This is an association that has planted 900 churches across America using the same model that we first used here at Church of the Highlands 18 years ago. We train about 1,000 church planters each year and give away about seven million dollars annually to help plant churches. My vision is for our church to be a model church with principles that are both transferable and *scalable*, so it can be done in a large church or a small church in any culture."

When Hodges describes his church in multiple locations, he includes several more in the pipeline. These campuses are built without any capital campaigns or fundraisers. His church is totally debt free, which allows them to do everything with cash. They can be aggressive in their generosity to plant or help grow new churches. Hodges explains, "We are not trying to break any records; we are simply leading people at the speed of their participation and generosity."

Hodges explains, "From a business standpoint, I've always thought things could be done differently in church, especially when it comes to money. Instead of asking for money, we operate our church finances the same way we should operate our individual finances. We should never spend everything we have."

Hodges said, "I am not against debt, but I am against getting addicted to it." He said there were times when the church had to borrow. When the church had a $30 million construction project, it had only $16 million saved. They borrowed and paid it off as soon as possible. Now they are debt free, so they build with cash.

Each new year the budget is 90 percent of the previous year's income. That means there is an automatic 10 percent margin in the coming year. That gives money for crises or tragedies and the projects with the most need. Borrowing restrictions in the budget automatically keep them from going into debt. The total church budget is over 130 million dollars annually.

A disciplined church grows out of the disciplined lifestyle of its leaders. Hodges testified, "I am constantly learning from churches that do things better than us. I had to grow in my speaking and leading. I had to grow spiritually. I had to grow biblically."

When it comes to personal discipline, he is faithful to keep personal Sabbaths and to honor family time. He is intentional about breaks because he knows his limits. He has people speak into his life about his schedule, travel decisions, and ministry projects. Finally, he wants to stay humble, not to think too much of himself or promote himself too much. He remembers his dad's pastor saying, "A man on his face before God cannot fall from that position."

When launching new sites for Highlands, Hodges uses the same eight principles that ARC uses in church planting:

1. You have to prepare the area spiritually through prayer and fasting.
2. You have to build a great team.
3. The location is absolutely critical.
4. How you communicate the launch is imperative.
5. Timing—some seasons are better than others. Not all months and weeks are the same.
6. You cannot give people a lesser product that what they get from the "main campus."
7. If you finance it heavily in the front end, it actually ends up being cheaper.
8. Do fewer things extremely well.

Hodges notes, "There definitely is a *formula* for the 12 cities we are considering right now. All of these future churches have to be a 'yes' before we do it. We like to begin the church in a portable, usually rented venue where the overhead is very low. It will take about 20 percent of the church's income to run that church, so that all other money is leveraged toward the future. We stay portable for about six years and grow to five services with about 4,000 people before we build a permanent location."

Hodges feels some churches build too small and put so much money into it that they don't have money for ministry. Hodges counsels that it requires patience to grow a church.

When asked to explain the church's growth and success, Hodges also gives four key ingredients. First, the God factor—he feels most would be surprised if they knew how much emphasis they put on prayer. Second, the life-giving system delivered in their ministry to people. Third, the right team—when the right people are together, they can do great things. Fourth, the right culture. If it is not life-giving, nothing will work.

The church has almost as many people in small groups as attend Sunday worship. Small groups exist to help bring people together. The Growth Track is where they discover their purpose in life, and then find a place on the Dream Team to use their gifts and talents to make a difference.

Hodges was asked to measure the effectiveness of his church. "Success for us is moving people from where they are to the place God intends them to be." His church makes this happen by providing opportunities for each person: "to know God personally, find freedom from the past, discover their unique purpose in life, and then do something that makes a difference in life." These four steps or principles are the foundation to individual success, which leads to church success.

DREAM CENTER

The vision for each Highlands campus is to build a Dream Center in the community where their campus is located. Dream Centers are designed to reach communities with the love of Christ by meeting both physical and spiritual needs.

As an example, the church purchased and renovated buildings in the Birmingham area to open both a Dream Center for community activities and a health clinic (Christ Health) to provide health care, dental care, counseling, and pharmacy services to serve more than 30,000 patients annually in the area.

PRISON MINISTRY

More than 2,000 inmates in correctional institutions worship with Church of the Highlands every week and participate in small groups. In addition to its work in the prisons, the church's ministry assists thousands with a re-entry program that sponsors ready-to-work initiatives. One day recently at Bibb County Correctional Facility, over 100 inmates were baptized in a single day. A commentator from the prison posted, "The purpose of prison should be to rehabilitate...what better path...than this declaration to God."

Worship services and small groups are held in 19 correctional facilities across the state. Those who minister to prisoners are trained before they are sent out to the correctional facilities.

There are also written requirements of what each can do or not do before they minister in the facilities.

The success of the church's prison ministry is seen in Mayo Sowell, one of the pastors at Highlands who had been in prison for selling drugs. Mayo thought he had it all because he played linebacker at Auburn University with the 2004 SEC Championship-winning team that went 12 and 0. He was recruited to the NFL, but an ACL injury cut his professional career short. He didn't know what to do and hung out with the wrong crowd. He tells other youth, "I had no thought of doing right...and I didn't want to go to church." He was sentenced to over four years in prison for selling drugs.

During his first few months in prison, he showed some interest in Islam, but his locker was stuffed with cigarettes and adult magazines.

Sowell explained, "While I was sweeping on a work detail, a prisoner I didn't know told me, 'There is an enormous call on your life.' I didn't know what that meant. He looked around to make sure no one was watching, then he prayed over me. Everything changed at that moment. The change was instantaneous and overwhelming because my heart was hungry. I had no job, no possessions, no plans...I had nothing to lose."

He immediately cleared out his locker, began living by prison rules, not his own, and listened to God. The man who prayed over him is Arthur Smotherman, and they are close today. Smotherman gave him a Bible and he spent hours poring over Scriptures with Sowell.

Sowell tells youth, "Help is just a relationship away. I met a man in prison who became my friend and changed my life. God placed that relationship there for me. It is what got me out of prison."

When he was released, he wore an ankle monitor while living in his parent's home. He could only travel within five miles, and the closest church was the Grants Mills Campus of Church of the Highlands. As he sat in the service, he felt accepted by the church and accepted by God, despite his ankle bracelet. The church changed his life.

He was invited to a small group but told them he couldn't come because of the bracelet on his ankle. "We can fix that," the leader said. The small group came to his home. Before long Sowell was leading small groups.

Once the ankle bracelet came off, Sowell testified, "Chains began falling off me spiritually...my mom, my dad, all started serving the Lord at Church of the Highlands."

Chris Hodges invited Sowell to a luncheon at Highlands College. The pastor asked everyone to share their dream. In that meeting Sowell said, "I saw that Pastor Chris had an uncompromising love for Jesus."

Two people in the church got Sowell a scholarship to the college because the unique goals of the college fit Sowell's call. Highlands College offers biblical education with a focus on hands-on ministry training, leadership development, and placement opportunities.

Sowell learned the purpose of worship at Church of the Highlands. "We are trying to get every person who hasn't been to church, or may not be a believer, to get them there and to come back...to experience Jesus." He adds, "I would have missed my purpose in life if I had not gone to Highlands College."

Now Sowell testifies at church and in public school assemblies, "To think people used to come see me for my talent playing football; now they come to see me for hope."

THE FUTURE

Chris Hodges talks about the future, "We'll keep on building life-giving churches in every community in Alabama. I want to see over 40 campuses launched in my lifetime."

Chapter 2

BUILDING ONE OF THE LARGEST
Faith Ministries

Hillsong Church Ministries
Sydney, Australia
Brian Houston, Pastor

The faith of Brian Houston built one of the largest Christian ministries in the world with over 150,000 worshipers and its influence through church planting, television, and social media. Houston also founded Hillsong music, Hillsong International Leadership College located in several nations around the world with students representing 70 countries, and Hillsong TV Channel is seen in over 180 countries.

Hillsong Church was planted by Brian Houston and his wife Bobbie as the Hills Life Christian Center in Sydney, Australia, in

1983 with 45 worshipers in the first service. Today, Hillsong has the largest number of worshipers in the world. Their average Sunday worship is estimated at 150,000 to over 200,000.[1] But after careful examination you don't know if it is a megachurch, a denomination, a huge Christian enterprise, or a movement. Perhaps it is best described as a ministry movement that has spawned megachurches around the world, i.e., 123 Hillsong locations (i.e., parishes) in 24 countries with almost 150 million worshipers with major Hillsong churches in New York, London, Paris, Sao Paulo, Cape Town, Kiev, Stockholm, Oslo, and Phoenix. The Hillsong television channel beams its message to 183 countries, or to at least 164 million households worldwide.

WORSHIP IS WHY IT GROWS

What is one word that best describes the extraordinary success of an Australian church in a land that is not known for vibrant evangelism? That one word also describes the phenomenal response across national boundaries, cultural divides, and denominational difference—*worship!* To describe it best, Hillsong is *worship!*

Houston explains, "God graced our church with a ministry of praise and worship that has exceeded our natural abilities."[2] He goes on to describe, "Worship is the strategy by which we interrupt our preoccupation with ourselves and attend to the presence of God."[3]

Houston is very quick to let you know worship is not just praise to God in contemporary music, it is not laughing or dancing, and it is not a method. "Worship cannot...be led from the platform. Worship must be an environment we cultivate, a culture we encourage..."[4]

When listening to the worship at Hillsong praise God, Houston commands, "I believe the sound of the house will always reflect the soul of the house. Where there is a healthy sound, filled with life...praise...adoration of God...there will be a healthy soul."[5]

To make sure you understand the transforming power of worship Houston said, "Worship is the overflow of what is going on in our heart."[6] Looking deeper into the heart, Houston says, "Worship has the power to write the story of your life."[7] Then to tie the two ideas together he says, "The same way worship does that to a room, I believe it can do it to your life."[8]

Then Houston changes the focus from what it does to the individual to focus on the cause for the personal transformation, "People begin to worship Christ as He is revealed to them...true worship comes out of a revelation of the One whom we worship."[9]

Brian does not discredit past worship; he notes, "There is a beautiful reverence that comes from singing the old hymns penned by Wesley and Newton...yet there is something powerful about new songs."[10] "The new worship is powerful because it is speaking to the here-and-now."[11] Houston says we can never move forward out of *"what we used to be."* We only move forward from *"where we are"* and *"who we are."*

Therefore, the secret of Hillsong success is that worship breaks down walls that divide. He mentions the age-old denominational divide.[12]

WHAT IS HILLSONG?

Brian Houston was born in New Zealand, attended Bible college there, and met his wife Bobbie at a Christian convention and was married in 1977. He served as assistant pastor to his father Frank Houston in New South Wales, Australia. When he saw a need for a church in the northwest suburbs of Sydney, he started Hills Life Christian Center in a rented public school in 1983. Houston pictures the Hillsong movement as "one house, many rooms." This is a description he gets from his wife Bobbie: "Hillsong is a single house with many rooms."[13]

Brian Houston was president of the Assembly of God denomination that was eventually named Australian Christian Churches (ACC). But in 2019, Houston left the ACC to form Hillsong into its own international denomination. Why? He answered, "The ACC has no idea who our pastors are around the world." He explained that the new denomination will "be able to issue credentials to our own pastors."[14] Today, the two organizations operate in good fellowship. Houston went on to add, "Denominations are (not) as important as they used to be. I think relationships between churches are so much more important than denominationalism."[15]

HOW HILLSONG GROWS

What makes Hillsong unique? What makes it attractive so that it is growing? The movement has an attraction to youth. It is more than the upbeat music, and more than the atmosphere, although those venues reflect the passion of the movement. Brian Houston is dedicated to three things—preaching about Jesus and His gospel; listening to the Holy Spirit and living supernaturally a life that is accessible to all, from the traditional church member to the skeptic and doubter.[16]

This attraction of Hillsong comes from their commitment to live out the Bible. Too often people read or study only one page or chapter of the Bible. Houston says, "If you read only a few pages you only see a few things from one point of view, but when you read the whole Bible it is like looking at the whole tree. One thing that stands out for me, from Adam and Eve all the way through, is obedience...when people are obedient to God, He blesses them."[17]

When you look at a Hillsong, the audience seems to be a crowd in their 20s and 30s, although that is misleading. Because many older believers are caught up in the energy of worship and the rush to Christian experience, they dress, act, and worship like the young crowd.

So what is the core of Hillsong? "At its core, Hillsong is devoted to preaching the gospel, listening to the Holy Spirit, and living supernaturally." This is accessible to everyone. "It stems from a commitment to living out the Bible."[18]

Brian Houston said, "The secret of Hillsong's success has been making Pentecostal theology accessible, even attractive to people who might be otherwise be turned off...by Charismatic elements." He says *worship* is the one element that has broken down walls between denominations, national cultures, and the difference between the rich and poor, the educated and those without education. "Worship has drawn great groups of people from the various parts of the Body of Christ."[19]

Because they want everyone to hear the gospel, when they come in the doors they are accepted, come as you are. Every person whether rich, poor, famous, unknown, or anything in between, they make sure they hear the gospel.

Brian says, "People are always looking for a way off this toxic highway that culture is giving people. But there is nowhere to go. So my job is to create local churches that are right there off the highway—you can see them a mile away."[20]

MINISTRIES OF HILLSONG

Music Ministry of the Church

Hillsong Music Australia is the hub of its ministry. They have released almost 75 albums with sales into the millions distributed in 90 counties. They have produced chart-topping albums from Hillsong United (youth) and Hillsong Live (worship) that involve their entire musical teams. Each year they produce Hillsong Live, an album of their music that is sung by congregations worldwide. Their most popular songs coming out of the movement are "Mighty to Save" and "Shout to the Lord" (featured on the television show *American Idol*).

Hillsong International Leadership College

Today, it is known as Hillsong College but was launched in 2010 with 550 students. Today it has numerous campuses across Australia and other nations of the world, plus Phoenix, Arizona. The college also offers courses online, offering diplomas, bachelor's, and master's degrees. It is accredited in Australia, with academic credit transferable to several of the best-known Christian universities in the U.S. Its emphasis is leadership training, but it also offers technical majors in creative arts, media, and artistic expressions. Both the student body and alumni represent over 100 nations.

Television

Brian Houston is host to a weekly television program, *Brian Houston TV*, seen in over 180 countries every week. He also airs another weekly program, *Let's Talk with Brian Houston*, seen both internationally and on Hillsong television channel.

The Hillsong channel is seen in 180 countries worldwide and is a joint venture of International Hillsong Church and America's Trinity Broadcasting Network (TBN), and can be seen on Direct TV, channel 371 (US), Dish Network, channel 258 (US), Glorystar (North America), channel 115, Sky in many nations, ABS1 India, and the Middle East, plus Hot Bird Satellite to Europe, and Agile 2 in Asia and the Philippines.

Hillsong Leadership Network

Their podcast was launched in 2016 and quickly jumped to the top five in religious podcasts with its Christian ministry. This teaching gives leaders around the world an opportunity to connect with Hillsong leaders and leadership teaching from Brian Houston and some of the other Christian leaders of mega ministries around the world. The Leadership Network sponsors open houses, luncheons, and informal gatherings around the world.

Hillsong Sisterhood

Bobbie Houston is the leader and mentor to the women of Hillsong, generally supports the traditional role of wife and mother, but also supports the church's position to "empower" women. Many describe the women's ministry as moving women from being a timid woman into leadership roles at Hillsong. Sisterhood takes on issues like HIV, domestic violence, and human trafficking.

Bobbie's leadership for women came from the "Pentecostal under-standing of spirit empowerment."

Hillsong City Care

Hillsong City Care has been established in many cities where Hillsong ministries include counseling services, health care, youth mentoring, and personal care program. It works within the communities to feed, clothe, and provide for the homeless.

Belief

Hillsong beliefs are traditional Evangelical and Pentecostal beginning with the belief the Bible is the authority in faith and life. They believe in the Trinity of Father, Son, and Holy Spirit and that Jesus Christ is the only begotten Son of the Father, whose death and resurrection provided forgiveness and new life in salvation for all. A person can be transformed by repenting, believing, and sub-mission of life to Jesus Christ. They teach the baptism of the Holy Spirit, and the Holy Spirit gives supernatural gifts, which include but are not limited to speaking in tongues.

Hillsong Young and Free

Hillsong Young and Free is a brand that has been successful in adapting worship and ministry to postmillennial youth worshipers. They especially include dubstep and electronic music.

Hillsong Kids

This contemporary ministry produces children's songs and albums. The album *Jesus Is My Super Hero* and *Super Strong God* were included in "Best Christian children's album" lists for several years. Also, *Hillsong Kids* releases an annual worship music album for children that includes live music recorded from Kiev, London, and Sydney.

Hillsong Conferences

Mid-year weeklong conferences are held yearly in Sydney, London, and New York. This is the largest gathering in Australia. The conference is led by Brian and Bobbie Houston and includes a variety of Christian leaders from across the globe. Delegates experience Hillsong and they become "messengers" to plant Hillsong back home.

HILLSONG NEW YORK

The future of Hillsong might be seen in a Hillsong church planted in New York City. The reasons the New York church has thrived are an indication of how other Hillsong churches thrive around the world.

Pastor Brian commissioned a young Carl Lentz who was ministering at the Sydney church to go plant Hillsong in New York City. Lentz was originally from the United States. Houston wanted to plant a Hillsong church in the U.S., but he understood the difference in culture. Today, the church in NYC has 6,000 worshipers, and the following is a glimpse into the reasons for success in foreign church plants. Brian gave him this vision: "I am not going to tell you what color to use. I am not going to tell you what style to use. The (Hillsong) framework has to remain the framework. This is who we are. This is our culture. This is what we believe. But within that, that is why I picked you. You know things that maybe I won't know."[21]

When you think of Hillsong in New York, you have to realize the celebrities who attend, worship, and testify of their experience of regeneration. It is a crowd of athletes, Carmelo Anthony, Jeremy Lin, and Kevin Durant (who was baptized in a pool on a New York high rise roof top).

Also, Hollywood celebrities include Justin Bieber, Hailey Baldwin, and Selena Gomez. There is reserved seating for these celebs.

In New York, Hillsong doesn't have a permanent location—no stained-glass windows, pews, or sanctified altar. Hillsong New York uses a mix of locations, a church on 22nd Street, Irving Plaza in Union Square, event space in New Jersey, and the Hammerstein Ballroom. For the millennials without a Hillsong in their area there is an app for worship, as well as the 24/7 Hillsong digital channel, including access to worship with acoustic communication, including BTS (behind the scenes) footage from a Hillsong conference, and even coffee time with Pastor Brian Houston online, Café Theology.

The church considers jeans "Sunday best" with casual tees and hats (to show off the fresh ink). No suits, ties, and Sunday dresses. Worshipers don't need a Bible; they follow the message with their iPhone. As traditional churches see Sunday crowds dwindling, Hillsong has beach day at Santa Monica Pier, food trucks at baptismal after-parties, light shows, and there are happy times when beach balls are thrown into the crowd.

Carl Lentz said, "When you say the word *supernatural*, what do you think?" He explains, "When you break down the word, it is *super-natural*, it is just 'natural' with 'super' on it. That explains Hillsong. It means everything is enhanced, everything is better, but it is still natural...it is not something you possess; you have the right to access it anytime you want." He then explained, "Supernatural is not a place you visit. It is presence you live with."[22] This is *indwelling faith*.

Notes

1. This figure is not verified, and it may include people who view worship by media (internet or television), or may include those who attend all their services, but worship is not connected by media.

2. Quoted in James Davis and Leonard Sweet, *We Are the Church* (Orlando, Florida: Billion Soul Publisher, 2014), 169.

3. Houston, Brian. "Creating a Worshipful Environment," June 7, 2013, https://hillsong.com/collected/blog/2013/06/creating-a-worshipful-environment/#.XbcM8WYpCUk (accessed October 28, 2019).

4. Ibid.

5. Ibid.

6. Ibid.

7. Ibid.

8. Ibid.

9. Ibid.

10. Ibid.

11. Ibid.

12. Ibid.

13. Berglund, Taylor, associate editor. "Brian Houston: How Hillsong Grew from a Small Local Church to an International Movement." *Charisma Magazine*, April 2019. https://www.charismanews.com/world/75791-brian-houston

-how-hillsong-grew-from-a-small-local-church-to-an-international-movement (accessed October 28, 2019).

14. Ibid.

15. Ibid.

16. Ibid.

17. Ibid.

18. Ibid.

19. Ibid.

20. Ibid.

21. Ibid.

22. Ibid.

Chapter 3

USING SOCIAL MEDIA
to Build a Church of 100,000

Life.Church, Oklahoma City, Oklahoma
Craig Groeschel, Pastor

The faith of Craig Groeschel built Life.Church into the largest attended church in the U.S. with over 100,000 worshipers in 40 campuses across America and influencing millions through social media and television. Pastor Craig Groeschel planted the church in a two-car garage in Oklahoma City in 1991 and has produced the YouVersion Bible app with over 375 million downloads.

Craig Groeschel, founder and lead pastor, began Life.Church in 1996 in a two-car garage with a handful of people. He testified that he did market research of non-churchgoers and designed his church from what he learned. The life approach was successful because the church began growing and today is the largest attended congregation in the United States with over 100,000 people in 32 multi-sites in 33 cities stretching to 10 Midwest states. But they are centered primarily around central Oklahoma.

Outreach Magazine announced Life.Church was America's most innovative church in 2007, which included free programs of sermons, transcripts, videos, and artwork. A team developed a modern translation/paraphrase of the Bible, *YouVersion*, a Bible app, which has been downloaded over 375 million times.

From the beginning, Groeschel planned to start a new and different approach to ministry, but the doctrinal core of Christianity was not changed. Its clear message was to lead people to become fully devoted followers of Jesus Christ. Weekly attendance grew and they began meeting in a local middle school. The next move was to a renovated bicycle factory; with continued growth, the only option was to add additional services.

In 1999, the congregation moved into a completed 750-seat worship center. Later that year it used its first off-site experience meeting in a movie theater. Some noted popcorn was included. By the next year they reached 3,000 in attendance.

The church had been named Life Covenant Church, but merged with nearby Metro Church, a non-denominational church in Edmond, Oklahoma. Then it had two campuses in Edmond and Oklahoma City. It combined the two names into Life.Church. The staffs from each campus were combined, and Groeschel became the lead pastor. In the early years of the merger, Groeschel commuted between the two campuses to preach live. Eventually, he was preaching five sermons Saturday night and Sunday morning. When Sam, his fourth child, was born in 2001 he was unavailable for the Sunday service, so the church used his previous Saturday night's video message on Sunday morning. He found this was not only acceptable, but popular with his different audience. From that experience, the video venue was initiated and put into multiple new plants in multiple locations. Groeschel doesn't claim to be the first to use video venues. He heard of another church doing it and with experimentation found it worked. This innovative breakthrough was the method that was foundational for growth.

The church practices what Groeschel calls "irrational generosity." In the early days he found other churches were interested in using the messages, videos, and kids' curriculum from their ministry. At that time, most churches practiced charging a small fee for providing these resources. Life.Church was especially having a hard time financially making ends meet, but when they started to freely provide their resources they found the Lord blessed the church financially. Now they offer the *YouVersion* Bible app free along with other church material.

When Groeschel was asked by the local press, *The Oklahoman*, how he measured success, he originally answered, "It is difficult to measure success...spiritually." Then he said, "So we measure what can be measured. We focus on what we believe helps people grow spiritually. For example...using gifts to serve...helps people grow spiritually. So we measure success by the number of people who are engaged in serving—both in the church and in community."

Groeschel looks for spirituality in people. "People grow better together in community than in isolation, so we measure how many people are involved in small groups." He added, "Since God calls us to reach out to those who don't know Him...we pay attention to how many people are visiting and the number of people who are new to the faith in Christ."

"From the very first weekend we met, in every gathering...we invite people to become followers of Christ. People who find faith new life in Christ are often excited...they cannot help but share it with those around them, including many who don't yet follow Christ."

When it comes to goals, Groeschel says, "We have no secret plans...our plans are pretty public and almost embarrassingly simple. We want to know God in all we do . . .We are passionate about building and releasing leaders...We are driven to help people discover their gifts and calling . . .We will do whatever it takes to reach more people. We have to do more of the same...open more churches...give more resources...build more leaders...see more people come to Christ.

"I have deep respect and love for my Methodist roots. I asked to start a church, but the denomination preferred more seasoned pastors...after being declined...I learned not to give up. It was difficult, painful, and embarrassing not to be accepted, but we can grow through adversity." *Crucible faith.* "This setback helped me become more humble, more teachable, and more resilient. Now, I am not nearly as afraid to fail. This is important...because when you are doing new things, you don't always succeed the first time."

The Oklahoman reporter asked if he was surprised at the report of being the largest megachurch in America. Groeschel answered, "We don't put too much weight on it or talk about it publicly. We don't feel we are a big church...we see ourselves as multiple communities of the Body of Christ working together. In other words, we don't see ourselves...a success...there is also much more to be done. Big organizations can be slow and bulky...lose their sense of urgency. With so many people left to reach...we prefer to see ourselves as smaller and we are hungry to do what God called us to do."

Following the success of using video sermons in their first two locations, the church launched campuses in Tulsa and Stillwater in 2003. Using video sermons guaranteed its future expansion. In the spring of 2006, they launched a campus in Fort Worth, Texas—the first church extension outside Oklahoma. In 2007, the church expanded further, opening campuses in Wellington, Florida, and Albany, New York.

In 2006, the church established an "internet campus" to broadcast weekly messages live over the internet, known as *Church Online*. A satellite uplink was built in the Oklahoma City campus so it could send a live video feed to all of its campuses. This revolutionary ministry provided a live worship experience for people around the world. This offered community to everyone, not just a worship experience to view. Worshipers everywhere were recruited to serve by being a part of a Life.Group and online mission opportunity.

Later that year, *Open* (aimed at churches) began. Through this media, Life.Church was able to share resources, creative content, messages (sermons), and resources. This service was extended to all ministries worldwide, completely free. That same year *Network Churches* was launched to partner with pastors and church planters who wanted to do the same ministry as Life.Church.

In 2007 the *YouVersion* of the Bible was offered as a free online Bible in beta version. The online worshipers could connect Scriptures with a wide variety of their online offerings. This included media content, pictures, video, blog posts, etc. By the end of 2007,

Life.Church was meeting in 6 states, with 49 worship experiences, and over 20,000 worshipers.

In June 2008, Life.Church invited hundreds of churches worldwide to pray, teach, and love as one in their first *One Prayer* event.

Then in 2009 several new resources and websites were launched including *Babelwith.me*, a real time chat translation tool; *Video Teaching.com*, a website with over 60 free video teachings; and the new *Lifekids.tv*. That year more than 2,000 churches from 38 countries united with Life.Church in One Prayer.

By May 2012, more than 2,000 churches registered to use *Church Online Platform*, a free web-based tool to help churches extend their ministry to reach people online. Also, over 900,000 resources were downloaded through *Open* for free by over 42,000 church leaders.

In 2013, the *YouVersion* Bible app was downloaded 120 million times. Also, the *YouVersion* Bible app for kids was launched in November with more than one million downloads in the first week. Church Metrics tracked 289,087 salvation decisions across all users. Also, over 25,000 people across the country were involved in Life.Groups across the country through Church Online.

Chapter 4

FAITH VISION
to Plant 100,000 Churches

World Harvest Center, Suva, Fiji
Suliasi Kurulo, Pastor

Suliasi Kurulo first had a vision to knock on every door on his island in Fiji to win people to Jesus Christ. Halfway through, Suliasi planted a church to help him reach every home on his island. Then he had a vision of planting churches and knocking on every door on every island in Fiji. He moved to Suva, capital of Fiji, to plant World Harvest Center, attendance now approximately 6,000. After planting over 300 churches on more than 300 islands, he began Christian Mission Fellowship International that has planted over 7,000 churches around the Pacific Rim, and now plans to plant 100,000 churches around the world.

I was 24 hours late in arriving in Fiji to preach at the World Harvest Center. My first plane was cancelled. Within an hour of landing I walked into the auditorium of the church. It was filled to capacity with 5,000 worshipers, another 2,000 sitting in the parking lot watching on a big screen. The atmosphere was electric, the people expected to hear a word from God. I prayed, "O God... anoint me...fill me...use me."

Right before I spoke a large Fijian woman dressed in a wrap-around sulu (sarong or pareau), began to sway to a hula dance and sing in English, "Jesus loves me, this I know, for the Bible tells me so." I loved her music because the presence of God filled the building. God was beginning to answer my prayer.

My sermon was on the Great Commission—planting churches. But not simply beginning a new church, it was "Planting Reproducing Churches." Every church planted must plant another church. The Great Commission teaches a cycle of church planting, and when that is done, we can complete the Great Commission in our life time and Jesus will return (see Matt. 24:14). What I was preaching is what pastor Suliasi Kurulo was already doing. He leads over 7,000 worshipers weekly, but more than that he is founder and president of Christian Mission Fellowship International (CMFI), which has planted over 7,000 churches across the Pacific Rim.

BUILDING FAITH IN A GROWING LEADER

Where does a great church begin? How does God prepare a man to reach the world for Jesus Christ by organizing a mission agency to plant 100,000 churches? It all began when Suliasi Kurulo stood over the open grave of his second son who had died at birth. Suliasi heard the words, "Dust to dust, earth to earth." A voice echoed through the sugar cane fields as he threw a handful of freshly dug soil over the small coffin of his baby boy.

Suliasi cried out, "Why, Lord? Why?" He had been doing everything for this child. But he continued to cry, "Why have you taken him away from us?"

Suliasi and his wife Mere lived in Labasa in the northern island of Vanua Levu, an island known for its friendship among the people and close-knit relationships between indigenous Fijians and those who came from the nation of India. The hardship of working in the sugar cane plantations had created a bond between these two ethnic groups as they harvested vast amounts of sugar cane and then replanted it the following season. Mere worked in the hospital and Suliasi was a young government employee in the public works department, a job secured by his degree in building and civil engineering.

Before the death of his son, Suliasi had been an evangelist part time knocking on doors telling people about Jesus Christ. But with the death of his son came a revelation from God that he was to change his ministry and purpose in life.

Pastor Kurulo had attended the international board meeting of the Ministry of Every Home for Christ in the United States. When the others at the conference heard about the birth, they give him a suitcase full of baby clothes. They joined in his and his wife's excitement.

Next, Suliasi had thought about a baby cot (crib) when he looked around his small house, but there was no money for the cot. Because he was an engineer, he even designed a cot, but he had no money to purchase supplies to build it.

Going through a shopping mall, he saw an exact replica of the cot, and he asked its price. He was told $120 dollars, "But we can give it to you for a special price of $100."

"Okay," he answered, "keep it for me."

Shortly after that, Suliasi received $100 and knew it was the provision for the cot. However, as a Christian he had always tithed. This was a challenge to his faith.

Suliasi told God, "I believe You'll provide the extra $10 if I first tithe." The store owner said he could pay for it when it was convenient, and when he looked at the bill it was $90. "This again confirmed to me God's leading."

But the baby boy died, and the cot was now empty, and so was the house. Suliasi prayed, "Lord, I don't understand. I was asking for a son. You provided everything for my son miraculously. Now I have a dead son."

As he cried before the Lord in his moment of grief, Suliasi heard the Lord speak,

"I also feel the way you feel, because I also have a lot of dead sons. I have provided everything for My children—I give them every spiritual advantage to enable them to walk in victory. But they are dead. I have no one to feed them and to care for them."

When Suliasi understood what God was saying, it was then he heard God say, "I am calling you into church ministry."

God was telling him to birth a church, to disciple, mentor, and teach those who had received the gift of salvation. Up until that point, Suliasi testified, "I had only been an evangelist and my passion was to get them saved." But from that moment on, his spiritual burden began to change to church planting.

Suliasi had not been trained as a pastor; he had no intention of starting a church. He had encouraged his new believers to go get involved in a local church, plus get under the ministry of Every Home for Christ.

Suliasi decided to conduct a survey among those he had led to Christ, asking if they would support the idea of a new church. Over 98 percent of the responders said, "Yes."

Suliasi thought he was too young to start or pastor a church. But again, God spoke to him, "Do not think that you are too young to be a pastor, because I have given you an apostolic ministry."

"At the beginning, I knew the call was a global call, but I did not know how it would happen.

"I began as a rural village boy, then I transitioned to living in a city where I went to school. I began to work, and now God is moving me into a global vision.

"God's vision will always have God's direction, and God's work will be done God's way, and will not lack God's supply."

WHERE IT ALL BEGAN

The strength of Suliasi's faith and vision was born into him as a simple village boy from a village of five clans representing 200 people. Without water and electricity, his water supply was a 15-minute walk to a nearby river.

He grew up in a wood-and-straw house with thatched roof and slept on a woven pandanus mat in the large open room; the only thing separating him from the hard ground was a layer of dry coconut leaves.

His father was a hard-working farmer with a herd of milk cows. From his earliest days he milked the cows for their extended family. If any milk was left over, he would walk two miles to government residences to sell them fresh milk. The walk crossed a winding creek five times.

He remembers waking up in the morning to the prayerful voice of his father who was petitioning God for all the relatives in the village and for missionaries around the world. God was planting a seed in his heart to evangelize the unreached people of the world. His father died in 2013. Until then his father was his most powerful prayer warrior. He testifies, "The seed of prayer planted by my father when I was a child has carried me through the years and has been a pillar for my life as a visionary leader and the founder of a church" (*second-generation faith*).

Suliasi faithfully attended Sunday school at a Methodist church each week about two miles from his home. He walked barefoot and the regular rain kept the road muddy. It became routine to stop in the creek to wash his feet and legs before entering either Sunday school or larger regular school.

One day they came to get him at school to take him to see his grandfather in the hospital before his death. Suliasi was his first grandson and namesake. The grandfather told Suliasi's father, "The church needs a proper church and my namesake is to be educated properly." The father agreed and promised to do it. Soon thereafter, his grandfather died.

Later, Suliasi learned that his grandfather had said to his sister, "From our seed, either your direct descendants or mine, will come a great man of God. I will not be around to witness this...great man of God." Suliasi draws a parallel to his grandfather and the last words of Jesus in the Great Commission, "Go...make disciples of all nations" (Matt. 28:18).

On New Year's Eve 1974, an evangelist came to the village to preach a revival. Suliasi was excited because he had heard this evangelist had been to Jerusalem. He testified, "Although I was going to church, attending Sunday school, joined the youth group, and regularly attended church, I had not made a personal commitment to Jesus Christ."

After the sermon the evangelist gave an invitation to walk to the front. He was the only youth to respond. It was the beginning of his personal journey with God.

That night his friends went out celebrating the New Year, but he had no desire to go with them. Later he testified, "A kind of peace flooded my heart and I didn't want to go anywhere. When I awoke the next morning, my friends were coming back from their all-night party but I didn't feel that I had missed out on anything...I was refreshed with peace in my heart."

Suliasi began school on another island, at Suva, the capital of Fiji. He remembers his first trip to Suva took almost a week because the boat stopped at every island along the way to load and unload cargo. He arrived early one morning to see city lights and new modern cars on paved streets. His father bought him new clothes, his first pair of shoes, and a new lunch box, and he stayed with relatives to begin school.

He attended for a while but was put out of school because the fees were not paid. Eventually his father heard and came to find him in Suva.

Suliasi was working with fishermen—mending nets and catching fish to sell for money. He thought about Jesus who called the fishermen to be His disciples and sent them out to "catch men" (see Mark 1:17). It is that passion he possesses to this day.

He had to return to his village, only to learn his father had given sacrificially to build a wooden church building in his village. After three more years in the village he left again for secondary school education.

After going through elementary school and the Suva Methodist primary schools, he graduated from the Fiji Institute of Technology, studying building and civil engineering, and worked briefly for the government.

TO THE REST OF THE EARTH

When Suliasi began building the World Harvest Center on Suva, he remembered a believer had spoken to him a prediction that the church would be shaped like an amphitheater. So, he told the architect he wanted the pulpit to be at the lowest level in the building to reflect leaders are there to serve and not be served. Just as Jesus reflected Himself as a servant by lowering Himself to wash feet, so the pastor of the church would be at the lowest level. Today when you walk into the church, it is a cone shaped auditorium, the preacher is looking up from floor level at the 4,000 people in a circular cone. Suliasi says, "As leaders we need to remind ourselves that we are here to serve God and the people, not to serve ourselves."

Suliasi said as he was praying about reaching out, God gave him the name of Christian Mission Fellowship. First, the word *Christian* identifies the movement with Jesus Christ who said, "I will build My church" (Matt. 16:18). The second word *mission* reflects seeking and saving those who are lost. The third word *fellowship* reflects the quality of relationship needed among the churches.

Suliasi is also founder and president of World Harvest Institute, a two-year Bible college in Suva, with six other one-year training programs in other islands of Fiji. They have sent out 7,000 missionaries to plant churches. The college is recognized by Oral Roberts University, Tulsa, Oklahoma, for the recognition of transfer credits.

The effectiveness of missionaries from CMFI is perhaps demonstrated by the lack of barriers they face while going into a foreign culture. His missionaries have an entry into economically poor countries, as Fiji is among the poorest nations in the world. Missionaries coming from Western cultures with their high standard of living have a more difficult time reaching some in the poor nations of the world because of the barrier between the rich and the poor, making evangelism difficult.

When CMFI missionaries went into Madagascar with its poor health, poor education, and poor malnutrition, they used rice farming projects as a major evangelistic outreach to the people. Rice is a staple ingredient of the population, so the missionaries used the project to provide jobs for the people. When they sold rice for income for their workers, it was also distributed for the nutritional needs of the people. Once the business was established, machines were purchased to prepare the rice for sale.

A storehouse was built in the mountains to house the workers, store raw materials, and to produce unassembled products to sell during the harvest season. During the off season, the people traveled as far as five days to the storehouse to buy rice. But even then, the gospel is always shared, and many give their hearts to Christ.

THE FUTURE

"Twenty-three years ago (1991) I had a dream that one day I would plant a Bible-believing, Christ-centered, spirit-filled, and mission-minded church. I had a dream that the church would own its land and buildings.

"I also had a dream that I would build a Bible school to train and equip workers for the entire world. I dreamed of building a Christian TV and radio station, and then a Christian printing press. After that I dreamed of a primary school, secondary school, and a university. I also dreamed that God would raise up millionaires in the church to fund the end-time harvest. But my dreams didn't stop there. I dreamed of building a need-oriented ministry that would minister to the physical needs of the people, as well as administering the Word of God to the spiritual needs of the people. I also dreamed that we would be completely debt free, and rather than borrowing money we would be able to lend to others and be a blessing to them."

Suliasi is convinced that when Jesus challenged "to the ends of the earth," his Lord was referring to the South Pacific. Suliasi points out that if you draw a straight line through the earth from Jerusalem to the other side of the globe, you come out at the Fiji Islands on the other side of the globe. He often encourages his congregation to recognize the connection between global missions and the command Jesus gave to go to the ends of the earth. As a result, his motto: "From the ends of the earth to the rest of the earth."

Technically, Fiji is located at the International Timeline or Dateline. Every new day begins in Fiji. Suliasi has often said, "If you want to know what God is thinking today, call me, because Fiji experiences each day before the rest of the world." With that understanding, Pastor Suliasi believes God has called him and the Harvest Center and CMFI to evangelize the whole world.

WRAP UP

When Suliasi Kurulo was a young man walking in an open field in his small village, one night he looked at the stars. The Lord spoke to him while he was praying. "This is the kind of ministry I am going to give you. You will see so many come to Christ, you will not be able to count them."[1]

The Great Commission has been his great ambition. Why? Suliasi says, "I am convinced that the Great Commission must be taken literally and seriously...we must go to the world—to the whole world—and preach the gospel to everyone. That means everyone has the right to hear the gospel."[2]

The second piece in the puzzle is the supernatural power of prayer. "To fulfill the Great Commission, prayer is the key that will remove every obstacle that hinders people from seeing the light of Christ."[3]

The third mandate includes ministering with other believers. "To fulfill the Great Commission will take the whole Body of Christ... it takes all of us working together to push back the darkness that oppresses lost people."[4]

The passion of the Great Commission still captures his heart.

Notes

1. James Davis and Leonard Sweet, *We Are the People* (Orlando, Florida: Billion Soul Publishing, 2014), 83.

2. Ibid.

3. Ibid.

4. Ibid.

Chapter 5

FAITH HAS PLANTED
Over 42,000 Congregations

The Redeemed Christian Church of God, Nigeria
Enoch Adeboye, Pastor

Enoch Adeboye pastors and leads The Redeemed Christian Church of God, Nigeria, to plant over 42,000 churches in over 180 nations of the world. Dr. Adeboye, Overseer of the church, earned a Ph.D. in mathematics and lectured in the university, but gave it up with the vision of planting a church within five minutes of each person in the inhabited places in the world.

Enoch Adeboye believes his church is God's focal point for God's ministry in the world. With great faith and vision, he states The Redeemed Christian Church of God plans to have a branch parish within five minutes of everyone in inhabited places in the world. An American RCCG pastor said, "To spread across America 'like Starbucks.'"

James Davis visited the monthly Holy Ghost meeting of The Redeemed Christian Church, Lagos, Nigeria, where over a million were in attendance. But beyond this enormous monthly gathering the church holds a Holy Ghost Congress once a year with as many as eight million worshipers, which might be the largest Christian gathering ever in a single place.

HISTORY

The Redeemed Christian Church of God was begun by Josiah Olufemi Akindayoymi, who was its first General Overseer. There were only nine people in the first prayer meeting. The founder was uneducated but was supernaturally endowed by God to read the Bible in his native language. On July 29, 1973, Enoch Adeboye was led to faith in Jesus through the ministry of Pastor Akindayoymi. Early on, Enoch Adeboye got his ministerial training by serving as an interpreter for the founder, also translating his sermons into English to be published. The influence of the founder was passed to the younger Enoch—*transferable faith*. The leadership mantle fell on the younger man in 1981 when the founder died.

THE MAN GOD USES

Enoch Adeboye was born March 2, 1942 to a poor family in Ifewara, southwest Nigeria. Poverty should have limited his influence, but early teachers called him brilliant with scholarly drive, and he was destined for academia. His family's poverty could have held him back. His family sold their goats and borrowed from neighbors so he could be admitted to one of Nigeria's foremost secondary schools, Ilesha Grammar School. He had an aptitude for books, especially science and mathematics. That directed his higher education to a bachelor's degree in mathematics from the University in 1967, a master's degree in hydrodynamics from the University of Lagos in 1969, and a doctoral degree in applied mathematics from the same university in 1975. His academic ambition flourished. His plan was to become the youngest university president in Africa, but God had greater plans.

He married Foluke Adenike Adeboye in 1967. He describes a wake-up call on his life in 1973 when his daughter became ill and was unresponsive to medicine. A cousin invited the couple to bring their daughter to a parish of the Redeemed Christian Church of God to seek divine healing. God answered their prayer. This professor of mathematics did not realize when they threw their faith in God how greatly God would change their lives. That experience was the beginning of God's ultimate plan for them and the Redeemed Christian Church of God.

The young mathematics doctor was ordained a pastor in the Redeemed Christian Church of God in 1977. He immediately showed passion for God's work by successfully pioneering Bible studies, crusades, revivals, outreach ministry and evangelistic programs. He was branching out all over southwest Nigeria.

In 1981, the founder passed to glory and Enoch Adeboye was given the leadership of the movement. Immediately, he left the academic commitment and set his heart on taking the Redeemed Christian Church of God to the next level. He directed his ministry to all social levels of the nation—from the poor to the rich, from the educated to those without education.

When Adeboye became General Overseer in 1981, there were 39 local churches in the western part of Nigeria belonging to RCCG. Within 20 years that number had grown to more than 3,000 with parishes in over 180 other nations.

ENOCH ADEBOYE'S MINISTRY

A book describing his ministry, *Pastor E. A. Adeboye: His Life and Calling*, states, "Everything that is happening at RCCG; nothing is of Adeboye at all...it is all of God."

The General Overseer testifies, "I cannot say I have any ability or wisdom. Everything has been the Lord Himself." Then he explains his position on the church's success. "God told me, 'I am using you as camouflage. People need to see someone. So, I am putting you forward so I can do My work from behind.'"

When asked the secret of his success, others observed he had childlike faith in the efficiency and power of the Word of God. His passion is to live a life of holiness, and teach others to also live holy lives. The core belief of RCCG is rooted in a life of holiness and obeying the mandate to preach the Good News around the world.

Adeboye says the pillars to success are vision and diligence. *Vision*—you must have a God vision that is bigger than yourself. *Diligence*—because the moment you begin to move forward obstacles will try to slow you down.

When facing the sexual scandals of some pastors Adeboye quickly answered, "Pastors must not take their anointing for granted, believing they are above sin." Adeboye who has been in ministry for 40 years used the example of Samson, who was a leader in Israel but fell into sexual immorality. He quickly added, "That is why I do not have a female secretary."

Adeboye says pastors cannot hide their sexual sins. "For there is nothing hidden which will not be revealed, nor has anything been kept secret but that it should come to light" (Mark 4:22). He noted Jesus said this will happen and if it is not true, then Adeboye said, "Throw away your Bible." That was his acknowledgement of the authority of God's Word. He said, "Don't wait to fight sin—flee sin." He points to 2 Timothy 2:22—flee *immorality*. He explains when a smiling sister comes to you in a "coy" way, run away in terror.

Enoch Adeboye has been careful to stay out of politics and not use his influence for political gain. Recently, a group of protestors staged a protest at Redemption Camp seeking Adeboye's intervention in political issues facing Nigeria. The security guards tried to stop them from entering, but they forced their way in to stage their protest. They wanted Adeboye to speak on their issue and use his influence with the government. The Nigerian Overseer of RCCG, Pastor Joseph Obayemi, spoke with them instead of Pastor Adeboye.

Adeboye responded to them, "Being quiet doesn't mean I am silent." What the protesters wanted Adeboye to say he had already indicated in the position and statements of Christian Association of Nigeria (CAN) and the Pentecostal Fellowship of Nigeria (PFN). RCCG is a member of both, and Adeboye is a past president of PFN. He did not want to speak separately from them, but he let everyone know he agreed with their position.

Over the years, Adeboye has traveled faithfully to minister first in the RCCG in southern Nigeria, and as new churches are planted around the world, he travels there to minister to them.

He stills preaches in remote African villages and in some of the largest churches in the metropolitan areas in the world. Those around him will tell you he has preached on every continent in the world. Note the following:

> He conducts a monthly Holy Ghost service (open air) in Nigeria with an average attendance of one million worshipers.

> He leads the annual Festival of Life in London, U.K., about 40,000 in attendance. He holds similar meetings in other cities around the world with attendance in the U.S. meetings averaging about 10,000.

> He leads the annual convention of the Redeemed Christian Church of God in Nigeria, U.K., Asia, and the U.S.

> His annually published devotional, *Open Heaven*, has sold over one million copies.

Everyone says Enoch Adeboye's humility is disarming. He easily shares his testimony with others. His passion for soul winning drives his church planting vision and prayers.

Because of his birth to a humble farming family, his life is characterized by the scripture: "Do not despise small beginnings." *Newsweek Magazine* listed him as "one of the 50 most influential people in the world." He has been married for over 50 years with three sons, one daughter, and many grandchildren. He lives at Redemption Camp, Lagos, Nigeria.

REDEMPTION CAMP

In the mid-1980s the Holy Ghost Service came into existence so that once a month the multitudes gathered for a night of praise, worship, prayer, soul winning, deliverance, testimonies and preaching. Initially these meetings were held in the ministry's headquarters in Ebute Meta, downtown Lagos. But they ran out of space. They purchased a piece of uninhabited forest land in south Lagos near Ogun State. It was a forest area filled with wild animals, which armed robbers used as a gathering place. This is now called the Redemption Camp, which is located on the Lagos Ibadan Expressway. The monthly Holy Ghost service is now held there with attendance of over a million worshipers. It has an open arena larger than Central Park in New York City. Adeboye built a home there where he lives with his family.

When Adeboye took over the church he established "model parishes," and over the years countless millions in the upper echelons of society have come to know Christ and worship Him. At the same time, the poor, needy, and downtrodden have not been ignored.

With millions of people flocking to Redemption Camp it takes thousands of volunteers to supervise, accommodate, and assist the flow of worshipers. People who drive to the meetings park two or three miles away, then walk to the arena. They have to arrive around 4:00 PM for the event that begins at 8:00 PM.

Redemption Camp has 5,000 homes, paved roads, banks, post offices, a mega power plant, supermarkets, giant warehouses, shops, restaurants, a fun fair (amusement park), and a police station. During the Holy Ghost service, people who don't live there year round sleep on mats in the massive auditorium and other parts of the camp. Worshipers surge to the arena for the three-hour service and the expressways leading to Redemption Camp are filled with shiny new SUVs, old rusty Corollas, packed yellow buses, and expensive limousines for the rich. All the roads are gridlocked coming from Lagos, which is 30 miles away. Many of those considered elite descend in helicopters to Redemption Camp's landing pad.

Christianity is widespread in Nigeria—especially the southern part—where you see Christian bumper stickers, billboards advertising against AIDS, religious symbols on clothing, and churches everywhere. Abortion is legal in Nigeria, but the majority of the people testify to the old saying, "Nigeria loves babies." Nigeria is addicted to "baby making." In a nation of over 160 million people, over 90 million identify with a Christian church, usually an evangelical church, but mostly Pentecostal.

One resident admits, "Where I came from people use their tractors to farm their land, here I use my tractor to cut my grass." Rubbish collection is continuous, not like many living areas in Nigeria that are littered with strewn rubbish.

The Holy Ghost meetings continue to grow. In 1998, over seven million attended this meeting and an observer communicated on television, "Not one person was lost or died." Now the church has a three-day Holy Ghost Congress every December at Redemption Camp. In addition to that three-day Holy Ghost Congress, a special program is held the first weekend of March as well. These events feature healings, signs, and wonders, and the power of God sets free (deliverance), anoints, blesses, and empowers.

As part of the Redeemed Christian Church of God's social responsibility to the community, they recently refurbished four police stations in the Surulere area of Lagos. Along with improving the physical facilities, they provided equipment including walk-ie-talkies, handcuffs, and other necessary items to keep the peace and prevent crime.

Enoch Adeboye gained international attention when he launched the first Holy Ghost Congress, December 18, 1998 in Lekki, southwest Nigeria with over 7 million people as reported by CNN and BBC. The two international news media reported it was the largest mobilization of people in one spot on the earth, a feat never before recorded.

The following year attendance at the Holy Ghost Congress grew to 8 million worshipers. This conference is held yearly in December at the Redemption Camp. From a one-night event in 1998, now it is a week-long event where people are won to Christ, plus God's moving power to "anoint and empower."

FUTURE INFLUENCE ON THE WORLD

Redeemer's University was founded in 2005, in Osun State, Nigeria, and is owned by RCCG. It has three colleges—College of Natural Science, College of Management Science, and College of Humanities. It offers undergraduate degrees, M.A., M.S., and Ph.D. programs. In 2013, the university was awarded a World Bank grant to establish the African Center of Excellence for Genomics and Infectious Diseases. It was ranked best university among 15 univer-sities in West Africa. Today it has almost 3,000 students.

Recently (2019), the Redeemer College of Technology and Management was opened at the Redemption Camp to provide leadership for a technological revolution in Africa by expanding the frontiers of scientific knowledge.

Worshipers in RCCG parishes around the country participate in the services by video; sometimes the program is beamed to parishes around the world. They announce gatherings as the largest attended single convention in the world. "It all has to do with the sincerity and dedication of the worshipers, and the humble leadership of Adeboye, or as they call him 'Daddy GO.'" But he attributes all the achievement to God.

The Redeemed Christian Church of God (not the denomination, but the local church) is the largest church in Africa according to the *Pew Research Center*, which also claims 82 percent of Nigerians are Christians. Pew researchers use the phrase, "Christianity is marching southward to develop the country." Pew identifies the growth of Christians in Nigeria with its growth in the Global South—South America, Indonesia, India, etc. Pew claims 60 percent of Christians in Africa attend church each Sunday, compared with 10 percent in Germany and 12 percent in the United States, those places where western Christianity is prospering financially.

Many are projecting that Lagos will become the largest populated city in the world with over 50 million people.

If that happens, what will happen to its churches? The ten largest megachurches in Nigeria all number in the thousands and millions. These ten churches are bigger than most of the megachurches in the United States.

The church broadcasts on a digital-cable channel called *Open Heaven* Television, Dove Television, and Liveways Network. Adeboye has written over 60 books and daily devotionals (Pen House distributes over a million copies annually).

TEXAS: WHERE EVERYTHING IS BIGGER

In the early 2000s, the RCCG bought 103 acres of land near Floyd, Texas, population 200. An hour northeast of Dallas you'll see a flat horizon, empty land, a few mobile homes and houses in Floyd. The church plans to purchase 5,000 acres and eventually build a 10,000-seat sanctuary, elementary schools, lecture centers, dormitories, cottages, a lake, and Christian themed water park. The church has already spent 1 to 3 million on over 500 acres and has expansion in sight.

Enoch Adeboye said he heard a voice from God to make Dallas the American center of the RCCG, but "you are not going to build a megachurch yet." God told him, "You are going to plant little parishes around the Dallas Metroplex and then I will give you a camp" (like the one in Lagos, Nigeria).

The leaders of RCCG see American Christianity has lost its way and is blinded by material wealth and pop culture. Therefore, America is a mission field; there are over 958 RCCG parishes in the U.S.

Last year the North American Convention of the RCCG held its annual meeting in Madison Square Garden in New York and drew an estimated 15,000 in attendance over three days.

RCCG CAME TO LYNCHBURG, VIRGINIA

I preached at the Lynchburg parish of the Redeemed Christian Church of God (RCCG), in 2018, to about 60 worshipers meeting in rented facilities of a strip mall. Six months later they are averaging over 80 worshipers and growing. Pastor Fola Ojuola moved from Nigeria to the U.S. in 2004 and planted the Lynchburg church in 2014. He represents the educated society that Enoch Adeboye has evangelized in Nigeria and is one of the many sent around the world to carry out the vision of planting a parish church within a 15-minute drive of people in this country.

In high school, Fola was invited to a Christian school fellowship. As a 16-year-old he went forward during a gospel invitation to give his life to Jesus. He was the first in his family to get saved. After earning a college degree in electrical engineering, he went to England for a master's degree in data communication. It was there a Pentecostal pastor told him, "You have a call of God on your life." He responded, "I don't think so." He testified, "All I wanted was to be an engineer." Yet in graduate school God began to talk to him about the call.

His wife, Olubukola (Bukky) Ojuola, studied medicine in Nigeria, earning the MD (doctor of medicine) degree. They met in college and were married in 1997 and went on a mission trip to Gambia, West Africa, in 2001. Both were working their secular occupations full time but spending all their spare time in mission work. Fola was ordained a minister in RCCG while serving in Gambia. At this time, they were sure God wanted them to do God's work, but they didn't know where or what.

At the end of three years in Gambia, Bukky came to the U.S. to add a master's degree in public health from Harvard University to her medical degree.

In December of 2006, Fola completed another master's degree in telecommunications engineering at the University of Maryland College Park. After living in the northeast of the U.S. working in the telecommunications industry and completing residency training, the family moved to Virginia. They then heard of a new medical school being started at Liberty University. By this time the Lord had put Lynchburg upon their hearts to go plant a church.

"Apply to Liberty's medical school," Fola said to his wife. He wanted to plant a church and she could teach in the new medical school. She was accepted as a member of the founding faculty in the School of Osteopathic Medicine at Liberty University. He planted the church in 2014.

LYNCHBURG FUTURE

What does the future hold? One family from the Lynchburg church is moving to West Virginia and Fola said his church plans to use that move to plant a new parish in West Virginia. Also he says, "I have to plant another church in the Lynchburg area."

Chapter 6

FAITH TO SYNERGIZE

2,500 Christian Ministries and 660,000 Churches to Complete the Great Commission by 2030

**Global Church Network,
Orlando, Florida
James O. Davis**

Faith to complete the Great Commission by A.D. 2030 by synergizing world influential ministries and mega-churches by: 1) communicating the vision of church planting in summits around the world to finish the Great Commission in our lifetime, 2) teaching how to get it done in online and residential courses, and 3) recruiting and sending world leaders to 800 Hubs to train resident workers in every nation to do it.

James O. Davis, founder and president of Global Church Network, Orlando, Florida, began coordinating churches and ministries in 1995 to actively seek to complete the Great Commission in our lifetime—by A.D. 2030.[1] He does this by training and motivating pastors, churches, and ministers to plant five million new churches for a billion-soul harvest. The movement first began as Global Pastors Network and later changed to Billion Soul Network® (its title reflects its goal). Finally, the name Global Church Network was adapted in 2017. Since its inception, the network has synergized its vision through two main sources—first, world influencing conferences, and second, by registering 65,000 pastors from around the world in over 200 courses both online and taught residentially in over 100 Hubs (800 Hubs by 2030) in major regions of the world.

DAVIS' CONVERSION AND CALLING

To understand the spiritual depth of this movement and its broad international influence, examine the faith of its founder. James O. Davis came to know Jesus Christ as his personal Savior on July 15, 1973, before cell phones, before computers, social media, and world travel by jet plane. Now he uses these tools to get the message out.

An invitation to accept Christ was given in his church to come forward and pray to receive Christ as personal Savior. He testifies, "I felt the Holy Spirit tugging on my heart and I was the only one who stepped out that morning to walk down the aisle and kneel at the altar to receive Christ as Savior."

The following summer at a youth camp James sensed a quickening of the Holy Spirit calling him into ministry. On Friday night when an invitation was given to spend special time in prayer, Davis prayed in the corner of the chapel and yielded his life to do whatever God wanted him to do. That night, Davis felt called to be an evangelist. While walking up the hill to an early morning teaching session, a counselor told him, "Don't run from the calling, run to it."

In high school James pitched for the school's baseball team. After practice one day as he was walking across an open field to go to his mother's car, the Holy Spirit asked, "What are you planning to do with the rest of your life?" He answered out loud to the Spirit, "To be a preacher of the gospel." The Holy Spirit responded, "Why are you spending so much time doing something you will never do?" That was his last day to play ball. From that time, he has focused on completing God's purpose for his life.

While a student at the Assemblies of God Theological Seminary, Springfield, Missouri, in 1984, Davis organized the nonprofit "Cutting Edge International." He wrote, "The purpose of Cutting Edge International is to fulfill the Great Commission." Cutting Edge International has been the parent company of everything the ministry and network has initiated and accomplished. Over the years, he has let that commitment guide him to step through any open doors that God has opened for him. Davis says, "You don't judge an opportunity by the size of the door, but by the size of the opportunity on the other side of the door." Little did he know the next opportunity behind the next door would be life-defining.

In 1993, the Assemblies of God General Council asked James to be the National Evangelist Representative to coordinate 1,500 to 1,800 evangelists. God was stretching Davis, and he ministered with some of the best-known evangelists in the Assemblies of God and also worked in some of the biggest churches in America and the world.

Then Billy Graham asked him to serve on the NACIE, (North American Conference for Itinerant Evangelists), where he learned how evangelists ministered in various countries of the world. He was being prepared for Global Church Network. The opportunities on the other side of that door were greater than the door itself.

In 1996, James Davis attended the National Conference on Prayer and Fasting in Houston, Texas and ended up in a prayer circle with Dr. Bill Bright, founder of Campus Crusade for Christ, the largest evangelical ministry with over 100,000 paid and volunteer workers. When James walked into the prayer circle the Holy Spirit said to Dr. Bright, "You will work with that young man who just entered your prayer circle."

On February 18, 2001, Davis left the Assemblies of God headquarters and arriving home, told his wife, "The wind of the Holy Spirit has changed direction today." She didn't understand. He told her, "Our lives will never be the same after today! Before 5 PM today, Dr. Bright will call me back and our lives will be different." Bill Bright phoned him by 5:00 PM and they agreed to fast together for seven days about a new initiative for pastors worldwide.

A week later James and his wife Sheri flew to the headquarters of Campus Crusade to launch the Global Church Network (formerly Global Pastors Network and Billion Soul Network). James explains: "Life is filled with *discovery*—discovery of new friends, discovery of new family, and discovery of new funds to get ministry done. Upon the heels of discovery comes new *development* of new opportunities—development of new emphases to preach and teach, development of new methods to get ministry done, development of new energy that motivates you. Then comes new ways to *distribute* to get new development out to the world—distribution online, distribution through persons, distribution through the churches. Finally, there must be *deployment*—deployment of your vision, deployment of your resources, deployment of people, deployment of strategy."

The above describes the strategy James Davis used to personally contact the most influential leaders of the world, bringing them together, holding worldwide summits, and instituting global Hubs. It is not uncommon for him to fly to any place in the world for a two-hour meeting with the right leader. James believes that the shortest distance between two points is not a straight line but a close relationship!

Dr. Bill Bright and James took a step of faith together in the twilight years of Bright's life to launch the Global Pastors Network (as indicated above; later became the Billion Soul Network and now Global Church Network) that envisioned a day when online training could be made available to pastors all over the world.

When the movement was getting off the ground, Bill Bright and James Davis released the book *Beyond All Limits*, which illustrates the strategy for completing the Great Commission. The book implied a "no roof and no walls" paradigm. When the roof is off there will be unlimited worship and unlimited flow of the Holy Spirit empowerment in the church. When the walls are down there will be no limit of connecting the local church to worldwide evangelism to complete the Great Commission. Global Church Network draws together synergistic churches with a mutual growing relationship with Jesus Christ where believers form strong relationships with both the saved and unsaved.

When they first announced an online training in 2002 at the Beyond All Limits Pastors' Conference, pastors and leaders kind of yawned, saying, "That is just blue sky." Dr. Bright and Davis saw a tsunami of technological training coming and were some of the first leaders to place training online for pastors. One well-known leader said that there would never be online training in Oceana in our lifetime. Today Davis is privileged to preach there and see digital technology up to and more advanced than U.S. churches.

Another leader said, "You will never be able to build synergy with the different streams of Christianity," and yet today there are 2,650 different denominations involved in the Global Church Network.

Davis recounts one late evening he was complaining to the Lord there never seems to be enough money to take care of the ministry. The Lord again quickened his heart, "Leaders with vision never have enough money, and leaders without a vision don't need money. The leader's role is to find a sense of timing to know how fast he or she can move in the vision along God's timing to provide growth. Tough times come when the leader gets too far ahead of the provision. Yet, even in the lack of good timing our mighty Lord provides for the need anyway."

The Billion Soul Initiative made its public introduction in September 2005 in Dallas, Texas, where 500 key leaders from 80 nations came together to focus on doubling the efforts of Global Church. Since that date new church plants by ministry members—and many other organizations—have planted 4.8 million new churches resulting in 940 million coming to Christ! In 2020, the Global Church Network will pass the goal of 5 million new churches for a billion soul harvest! Here are a few global statistics reflecting this growth:

> Chinese: 45,000 come to Christ a day

> India: 20,000 come to Christ a day

> Africa: 20,000 come to Christ a day

At the time of this writing, between 110,000 and 125,000 people are coming to Christ each day and more than 1,200 churches are planted per day.

Western Christianity in America and Europe has slowed in growth, and in many places western churches have plateaued or even gone down in attendance and membership. In the west it seems the influence of evil has grown, while the influence of righteousness has slowed. At the same time statistics show evangelism growth and surges of Christianity in the Global South (nations below the equator). Global Church Network works in all nations, but focuses in those rapidly growing nations.

REGIONAL SUMMITS

Global Church Network often begins by James flying to meet with one or a few leaders about the possibility of partnering together for a future national summit. Once there is agreement between key leaders, Global Church Network announces a strategic summit in the capitals or large metro areas of international nations inviting all Christian leaders and pastors to a three-day synergizing meeting where pastors from some of the largest churches in that country will join with speakers who are the conference leaders from some of the largest churches in the world. More than information and more than challenge, they develop a strategic plan to reach every area of that nation, including identifying areas where there are no churches and no portions of Scriptures in languages of unevangelized people groups.

From the beginning, Global Church Network has sought to jump-start worldwide evangelism through these regional synergistic summits across America and around the world. The plan delivers the urgency and credibility of completing the Great Commission. A number of international pastors and denominational leaders representing the largest attended churches in the world speak at these summits and conduct roundtable discussions. The reputation of these speakers attracts some of the most important delegates in each regional meeting. They come, not for what they get for themselves, but for what they could give. Davis challenges, "Let's together complete this Great Commission challenge in our lifetime. It is not enough to simply grow our respective ministries, but we must determine what will it take to complete the Great Commission."

AGGRESSIVELY FINISHING BY 2030 A.D.

Global Church Network launched the urgency of finishing the Great Commission by the 2,000[th] birthday of the Church, i.e., Pentecost. That's when Jesus gave the command to "Go into all the world...preaching to every person...making disciples in every nation," i.e., people groups (adapted from Mark 16:15; Matt. 28:19). This challenge is so great no church, organization, or individual can finish it alone. It takes all believers, in all churches, and all church ministries to work together to finish the command.

Why is Global Church Network so time-driven to finish Jesus' command? Because Jesus said, "The Good News about the Kingdom will be preached throughout the whole world, so that all nations will hear it; and then the end will come" (Matt. 24:14, NLT). Davis interprets this promise that when the gospel reaches every people group and some are saved, then the Father will tell Jesus in heaven, "Go get our people."

Davis is well aware that no one knows when Jesus will return "except the Father" (Matt. 24:36). Just as Jesus came the first time, "When the fullness of time had come, God sent his Son" (Gal. 4:4 NKJV), so when the fulness of time for the church comes, the Father will send His Son the Second Time.

Today, we don't know when the church will complete Jesus' command to evangelize all people (including people groups). Global Church Network is not predicting dates when Jesus will return. It is being motivated—aggressively—to evangelize all cultures (people groups) in the world. When the church does that, He will come (Matt. 24:14 NKJV).

The word *aggressive* describes the focus of Global Church Network. The following chart explains the necessity of attempting to reach the unevangelized people groups as soon as possible, with every method possible, using as many workers as possible, taking advantage of the times and quickly as possible.

AGGRESSIVELY COMPLETING THE GREAT COMMISSION

> Because Jesus commanded, "Go into all the world... make disciples of every people group" (Matt. 28:19 AMP)

> Because when the Great Commission is completed, Jesus will return (Matt. 24:14)

> Because the time is short to complete the Great Commission by a.d. 2030, the 2,000th birthday of Pentecost

> Because our love motivates us to obedience (1 John 5:2)

ORGANIZATIONAL FOCUS

Davis explains the important focus of the organization, "Christ wouldn't have asked us to do something we couldn't do!" Then he added, "Christ wouldn't send us places we couldn't go." And finally, he adds, "Christ wouldn't give us principles to get the task finished if He didn't believe we could complete the task. So what is left? We know where to go—everywhere on earth. We know what to do—plant churches that will plant more churches. We know when— now. So, let's find a role in God's goal and do it…. God's goal," says Davis, "is everyone. He is not interested in a percentage of the world but the entire world. Yet, no one or any single organization can reach everyone. Thus, we must find our role in God's goal and our part in God's heart."

Jesus said, "Do it" (see John 14:13), long before Nike said, "Just do it."

Davis acknowledges the dangers and controversy of evangelism in some parts of the world that are hostile to Christianity, where Christians are being martyred and churches are burned. He says, "I go to those dangerous areas to mobilize leaders and churches and lead ministry forums, prayer rallies, and regional rallies. Our speakers come from all over the world to show up in those places—all because Jesus commands us to go everywhere, all the time, being busy in all areas of ministry."

The goal of large international summits is to bring together international influential leaders to meet with the most influential leaders in that nation in strategic round-table initiatives. Part of the strategy is knowing who the unreached are, where they are located, and then how to evangelize them. Out of that summit or conference in each nation, they communicate the results in a "world mapping" presentation to challenge all denominations and churches with the unfulfilled goal. What is that goal? There are over 2.7 billion souls who don't have access to the gospel. Davis says, "It is our task to find them, point them out and challenge everyone to reach them by developing a strategy to get all saved, taught, trained, and discipled. Then it is our responsibility to take this information to their people so all can help reach all through church planting and evangelism."

NOT THE "WEST TO REST" STRATEGY

Davis articulates, "It is no longer the West going to the Rest but the Best around the World going to the Rest of the world." The pastors and leaders of some of the largest churches and ministries in the world work with Global Church Network. James O. Davis has ministered in most of these extremely large churches. He has ministered in 135 nations to date. Americans think a *big* church has an attendance of *tens* of thousands of attenders. But *big* churches around the world (especially the Global South), have *hundreds* of thousands in attendance or more.[2] They have massive budgets, wide outreach, and they influence their region and beyond. Leaders from some of the largest churches/ministries fellowship with Global Church Network from the following nations:

India (largest ministries in that nation)	Nigeria	Indonesia	Ireland
India (largest churches)	Uganda	Fiji	Netherlands
Nepal	Chili	New Zealand	Belgium
Ecuador	Ghana	Trinidad	Kenya
Argentina	Suriname	Philippines	Ireland
Belgium	Malaysia	Singapore	Italy

GLOBAL CHURCH LEARNING CENTER

The Global Church Training Center has over 200 courses taught by God's finest leaders from all over the world in the areas of leadership development, evangelism, discipleship, visionary networking, global missions, and church planting. Tens of thousands of pastors from all over the world have taken these courses.

Pastors from all over the world are registered in the more than 200 courses offered online and residentially. These courses are doctrinally sound, interactively engaging, and visually attractive. Rather than exposing students to everything on a topic, the most important information on each topic or subject is presented. If a student already has graduated from a college or seminary, they begin in the advanced studies program.

Those who teach represent some of the most outstanding leaders in the Christian world: Jack Hayford, president emeritus, Kings University; Glen Burris, President of Foursquare Church; Gustavo Crocker, General Superintendent, Church of the Nazarene; Doug Beacham, General Superintendent of International Pentecostal Holiness Church; Timothy Hill, Overseer of the Church of God; Leonard Sweet, faculty at Drew University; Kenneth Ulmer, pastor Faith Central Bible Church, Los Angeles, California; Howard Hendricks, former professor Dallas Theological Seminary, Dallas, Texas. I am the dean of this Learning Center. I am co-founder of Liberty University, and I teach several courses in both levels of The Learning Center.

GLOBAL STRATEGY REFLECTED IN ONE SUMMIT

In 2018, I joined James Davis and several other leading pastors from the U.S. and around the world. We flew to Kathmandu, Nepal (called the rooftop of the world). We were hosted by the Central Assembly of God, a multi-site church of 3,000 worshipers (the largest church auditorium, plus seven multi-sites). We called this event, "Give Me This Mountain Summit." We originally planned for 500 to 700 delegates, but over 1,500 delegates showed up. The parking lot was so filled with motor bikes, we could barely make our way to the church auditorium. The building had no pews; everyone sat on beautiful rugs, men on one side of the room and women on the other. We challenged every delegate to each plant another church like their church. We announced there were over 20,000 unreached villages across the Himalayan Mountains in Nepal. All the leaders adopted the goal to help plant churches in all of the villages of the Himalayan region by 2030. When the invitation was given, every delegate stood to pledge to plant churches across the Himalayan Mountains.

"Sit down," they were instructed.

The second challenge was given to plant not just one church but begin a church that would plant at least five more churches.[3] In essence, every delegate would plant one church that would reproduce multiple times, i.e., many new churches. They all stood again. That's a possibility of over 7,500 new church plants in the Himalayan Mountains in Nepal.

But challenges and promises are only the beginning process. Delegates were enrolled in online courses to plant new churches (GCN follows that pattern in new countries). But their online courses are not enough! After every Global Church Network conference, a regional Hub meeting was planned for that area. In less than two years, the first Kathmandu Hub has been multiplied into seven Hubs in every province. Teachers from the leadership team of Global Church Network will return to Nepal to personally teach intensive classes on church planting. These are "face to face" intensive classes. Following that experience each delegate is enrolled in more online classes that will eventually lead to graduation and a diploma. Visiting pastors will return to teach, supply role model examples, motivation, statement accountability, and a strategy to complete the task. The goal of Global Church Network is a commitment to the leadership of Nepal to plant a church in every unreached village across the Himalayan Mountains. If Global Church Network can do that in every nation of the world, the Great Commission can be completed by 2030.

THE FUTURE

Global Church Network filled the Castle Church, Wittenberg, Germany, November 1, 2017 to celebrate Martin Luther's 500th anniversary of the beginning of the Protestant Reformation. God gave favor, and approximately 760 different leaders from every nation came not only to focus on the celebration of the 500th year of Protestantism, but to focus on *Finish 2030*—finishing the Great Commission by the 2,000[th] birthday of the church. FINISH is an acronym for Find, Intercede, Network, Invest, Send, and Harvest. These are the six overarching steps that the Global Church Network believes are required to complete the Great Commission.

Davis announced, "We launched *Finish 2030* at Castle Church, a huge step of faith, but we believe God had given us enough denominational buy-in over the years to complete the Great Commission. We are now pushing forward to reach the hardest and the remaining 3,000 unreached people groups left in the world to finish the Great Commission by 2030."

Just as David the shepherd boy had to defeat the lion and the bear before he took on Goliath, there is a stepping stone process where God leads us from little things to bigger things. And as Davis looks back over the 40 years of evangelistic ministry he sees where little things were started and the little things the Lord used to give him more. He teaches, "We are called to synergize the best relationships, systematize the best training, and strategize for the remaining unreached people groups."

Notes

1. The date A.D. 2030 marks the 2,000 anniversary of Christ's death, resurrection, and the original giving of the Great Commission.

2. The largest churches in Nigeria, Africa have the largest sanctuaries of any in the world. Their weekly worship attendances in many cases exceed 100,000, dwarfing the vast majority in the U.S. or in Western Christianity. See a detailed list of global megachurches, sortable by sanctuary size, attendance, country, and other qualities at leadnet.org/world, compiled by Warren Bird.

3. Elmer Towns, *Planting Reproducing Churches* (Shippensburg, PA: Destiny Image Publishers, 2017).

Chapter 7

BUILDING AN INTERNET CHURCH
of 60,000 by Faith

**Glory of Zion International Ministries,
Corinth, Texas
Charles "Chuck" Pierce**

Charles "Chuck" Pierce, president and prophetic leader of Glory of Zion International Ministries in north Texas, reaches out to "scattered sheep" (members of his church), networking over 60,000 members into one church family. Today, the ministry includes individuals, House (churches) of Zion, Businesses of Zion, Ministries of Zion, and Street Churches of Zion.

Glory of Zion uses the internet to fulfill the Great Commission to weekly reach, teach, baptize, and train people worldwide. Some ask if online interaction can be a church if people are not gathered in one place. Is it a denomination? Is it a fellowship? Or a church planting agency?

Chuck D. Pierce, president and prophetic leader of Glory of Zion International, was assigned to "align" God's "scattered sheep" from around the world. His description of "aligned members" is a noun used by churches for "church membership." He gathers all kinds of believers from all different places and cultures of the world. Pierce took leadership of a small local church in Denton, Texas, and taught "core values" concerning the foundation of the church and the first principles of the Word of God, including Israel. This became the rallying cry in a movement that has now become an international online church. Some describe it as a Google denomination or a Google church. Dr. Pierce describes it as God realigning the Body of Christ to bring us into His call of One New Man, Jew and Gentile, in latter days (see Eph. 2:14-16).

Glory of Zion is made up of "aligned" members from home churches (begun by the movement) of approximately 1,200 believers from northern Texas, and then approximately 60,000 individual believers from all over the world. There are house churches, also Businesses of Zion (commercial) and Churches of Zion (pre-existing churches that have aligned and are tied together by regular internet connection).

Chuck visits his "flock" through world-wide conferences where individuals and groups come together for instruction, fellowship, motivation, and re-enforcement of purpose. Once every four to six weeks the staff spends a week praying for each person who is aligned with the ministry.

I asked Chuck Pierce why he began an online church. He answered, "I had always used the internet and was beginning to move into a wider communication structure with other social media. I had a desire to develop a world-wide prayer movement. I didn't originally think of developing an online church."

HOW GOD DEVELOPED AN ONLINE PROPHETIC LEADER

To understand the outreach of Glory of Zion, examine the salvation and call to the ministry of Chuck Pierce. Then look at the experience God used to equip him for this unique ministry.

When he was 11 years old in a Baptist church, they gave an altar call every Sunday to be saved or surrender to the Lord. He testifies, "One day I was sitting on the third row and actually I felt the Lord standing next to me when He said, 'Today is your day.' So I went forward and got saved.

"When I was 18, I was going through a hard time, because my dad had died. I ended up with double pneumonia in the hospital under oxygen. The Lord put me in a room with a Pentecostal pastor who introduced me to someone I did not know, the Holy Spirit. The Lord visited me, and I started devouring the Word of God. He spoke to me, 'I can restore your loss.' And my whole life has been about restoration since then.

"When I got out of the hospital, I went to the state Baptist convention in Dallas. As I was sitting in the congregation while they were ministering the Word, the Spirit of God spoke to me again, 'I have called you for the healing of the nations.' That call never left me.

"When I started college, I began with plans to end up being in the medical field. However, something had strategically happened when I went forward and wrote on the dedication card, 'I am called for the healing of the nations.' Still, I knew down deep that I was not to end up as a medical missionary in Ethiopia. When I left the altar, there was the most beautiful red-haired lady next to me named Pamela Hughes. She too had surrendered for full-time service to the Lord. A week later I asked her for a date, and we ended up getting married the next year. We have now been married 46 years. I have travelled to approximately 120 nations, and 47 years after receiving my call.

"When I transferred to Texas A&M, I shifted into operational management. I finished my degree and went to work in the oil and gas industry working in a new field of system design. I ended up being a part of a team that helped design the first human resource system. This was God's preparation for me to design a system at Glory of Zion to reach His other sheep.

"Five years later, my wife and I were at the top of Shell Plaza in Houston at a dinner when she looked at me and said, 'You know this is not what I really signed up for, and if you go much further you will be caught in this world the rest of your life.' That motivated me to pursue God in a new way. I had always been faithful in church and taught Sunday school. But suddenly, the Lord began to remind me of my call to the nations.

"Our church, Northwest Memorial Baptist Church, Houston, went into a huge building program and I was asked to become the administrator of that church to lead that program. That introduced me to full-time ministry. Northwest Memorial Baptist Church was one of the pioneers in the third wave movement, i.e., charismatic. It was also part of the home church movement. So that implanted in me the need for house churches throughout the world. When I finished that project, I became executive director of Boys Country of Houston, which was the second largest private children's home in Houston. Again, God was stretching me.

"Then the Lord visited me about the Soviet Bloc countries and gave me a download from heaven of what would happen in the future to the Soviet Bloc countries. That was in January 1984. God told me they would open up and that He wanted to have me ready when the churches became open to the gospel in the Soviet Bloc countries. God led me to work with Ralph Mann, head of the Mission Possible Foundation, and we worked with Brother Andrew. In November 1989, the Soviet Bloc countries opened up through the Romania revolt. Because the Lord had told me what materials we had to have ready for the churches, when they opened up we embraced the opportunity.

"The Lord brought me to Denton, Texas, to minister in a little church called Believers Fellowship. My wife looked at me and said this is the church we are going to attend. I had never been in a church like this. Robert Heidler, a graduate from Dallas Theological Seminary, was teaching in the church and was making a shift into the things of the Spirit. That small church, Believers Fellowship, has now grown into Glory of Zion International Ministries.

"Eight years ago, the Lord enabled the church to purchase the center that was a Boeing facility to manufacture cockpits for the 747-passenger jet.

"I started the online ministry in 2004. I had already worked with Peter Wagner since the 1990s in the prayer movement, prophetic movement, and with the new apostolic reformation. When I began sharing about online ministry, many questioned its role and I was even asked to explain this position before a group of 600 apostolic leaders. I got some flak even though people quickly saw we could reach the entire world through the internet and influence many through social media. It is our way of gathering the Lord's 'other sheep.'

"In the early '90s I went back to school and worked on my master's degree in cognitive systems at the University of North Texas. It was there I saw a system that could gather people from all over the world. I needed more than spiritual knowledge, and God gave me the technical wisdom to do it. That is really when this ministry started. I had always communicated with the church in Russia even before the internet was big. We had cryptic communication. I had learned a process of doing church that way, which I had actually used with some leaders in Russia, via the internet. Later, when Peter Wagner got me involved with the world prayer movement, I helped design a system that would allow us to communicate by prayer worldwide. My present assistant, Brian Kooiman, helped me develop that system. From there I was able to develop and gather people worldwide who did not fit in the normal church.

"Glory of Zion is really a universal church, but it is more than a church—it is a movement. Glory of Zion is a church ministry and movement tied together!

"I see a remnant arising in every nation. The remnant is our seed for the future. These are God's sheep being gathered together. I also see that Glory of Zion will be a part of the Lord's work of separating sheep nations from goat nations based upon who is really pursing the Lord (see Matt. 25:31-46). If there is a remnant house of prayer in every nation, some way or another, Glory of Zion will be connected to that ministry. The basis for our hope is Isaiah 56:7, 'I will bring them to my holy mountain of Jerusalem and will fill them with joy in my house of prayer. I will accept their burnt offerings and sacrifices, because my Temple will be called a house of prayer for all nations'" (NLT).

FOCUS ON SCATTERED SHEEP

Pierce thought deeply and explained, "The idea of an online church began during the first decade of this millennium when the Lord spoke to me, 'Gather the scattered sheep.' That was the word from God that He wanted me to focus on His 'scattered sheep' around the world. My question was, how can I do it? So, God said to me, 'Use the communication system that you are now using, use the internet and social media to gather My sheep.'"

Pierce said, "I didn't just want to broadcast a message to the 'scattered sheep,' I needed a relationship with them to effectively minister to them. God was instructing me to form a spiritual relationship that would attach them to the Lord and to one another, so they could grow in Christ."

When Pierce was asked *"Who are these scattered sheep?"* he answered, "These are people who have left the traditional church for many reasons, yet they still had a tender heart toward God and want to worship God."

Pierce went on to say that he has about 60,000 names in his database, but 30,000 highly invested Kingdom seekers. He regularly sent emails to them on his *prophetic* updates. He began his online church by asking them to align with him in a relationship, so they could receive a unique message about the body of Christ for them through him.

"I didn't understand how they would align, and I didn't understand what I had to do. As I continued to pray, God gave me a strategy for how to develop a new alignment by which we could become a community, i.e., a church.

"As a result of this strategy, I developed several areas where scattered sheep could align with us. The very fact that they are scattered means they need to be gathered. The very fact that they are scattered means that something in a local church drove them away or allowed them to drift away. Also, the fact that they were sheep tells me that they have a heart for God, but for some reason they were not in church.

"So, I determined first I needed a message that would bring them together. That was the message that God gave to me that would become the catalyst around which 'scattered sheep' would gather. This was the message that scattered sheep needed to know. God loves you, God welcomes you, God will embrace you, God will welcome you home, God will feed you spiritual food, God will build you up with instruction and teaching, God will use you in service, and finally God wants you to worship Him.

"Worship is the core of all we do. Worship is the glue that holds us together—from the top to the bottom, from the beginning to the end—worship involves all that we are and do.

"I determined that these scattered sheep must interact with one another and with our ministry, just as local sheep interact with a local church. So, I began developing a pastoral structure to align people together, to align them with the church, and to align them with our ministry. It was important to get shepherds to lead and feed the sheep before we began gathering sheep.

"I'm not sure that one man or one personality can pull together thousands of sheep or even millions of sheep. It takes many co-shepherds and under-shepherds and assistant shepherds to gather all the scattered sheep and feed them and minister to them."

Therefore, is this an embryonic denomination in the making? Or is this an independent Bible-teaching agency, or is this a church?

INDIVIDUALS ALIGNED

"There are five ways we have gathered scattered sheep and formed a new network for the Body of Christ, and this is through the internet. Just as people use the internet to relate, play, learn, shop, find love and marriage, so I believe they can pray, learn, fellowship, grow and live in a Body of Christ through the internet. We're not just looking for people to tune into us for a sermon or lesson as someone listens to a radio sermon; no, we want them to be aligned.

"That word *align* became a key word. Today we have over 60,000 people who are connected with this ministry. These people have attended classes online or here at the church in Corinth, Texas. They participate in our gatherings and prayer focuses and seek to implement the revelation the Lord releases through this ministry. Through this relationship they are connected with us... they are *Zion Aligned*. (This is similar to an individual joining a local church, or a house church, or resident church, or becoming a part of a Business of Zion.) We accept *Zion Aligned* people as much as any church would accept members. We commission our people by tying them to the core values of Glory of Zion International Ministries."

ZION HOUSE CHURCHES

"We have over 5,000 Houses of Zion, house churches. These are led by leaders who have aligned with our core values. When I say we have 5,000 house churches, we have started with 5,000 church leaders. But a house church involves a lot more people than 5,000 leaders; a house church includes all those who worship in their house. There are some house churches with 25 in attendance; some have only 2 in attendance. I expect house church leaders to be shepherds for these scattered sheep. Obviously, they are gathering new 'scattered sheep' into their house churches all the time."

When I asked Chuck Pierce how he could personally look after such a large number of house leaders, i.e., pastors, he told me, "God was showing me that the pastors are the key to these house churches. I serve the whole body *prophetically*, giving them God's Word by teaching, preaching, and exhortation. Then I serve the local body *apostolically*, meaning I must exercise the gifts of the apostles for the body.

"At the beginning of this millennium I realized that the traditional way of doing church was going out the window. I had to develop a new pastoral perspective to church. Therefore, I had to redevelop ministry.

"God began to show to me that I would minister to the people all over the world, and that it wouldn't be by radio or television; I knew it would be in a different format. Yes, I would still travel and do regional meetings where all our people come together. When that has happened, it has been a tremendous blessing to me, as well as to all of the people. That ministry builds up local churches.

These regional meetings are a way of keeping people connected to one another and connected to the ministry.

"But also, I needed the 'scattered sheep' to travel to northern Texas to be a part of the ministry by attending classes and experiencing what God is doing here in our corporate gatherings.

"Again, we are looking for people in the house churches who are no longer connected to a local church. Scattered sheep need a house church. They've been messed up by the church, or they've left the church out of disgust, and they are looking for a way to come back and align themselves with the Body of Christ.

"When leaders attend our various schools here in Texas, they are mostly taught by Dr. Robert Heidler who instructs along with me from a basic Hebraic perspective. We've had as many as 5,000 people connected to one of our schools through conferences online. We are doing church a totally different way than the average local church is doing it.

"Residential schools and online schools are the way people connect with Zion, and this is the beginning of a basic relationship between the people and the church. Even though we are an online church, we don't desire to just connect with them online. We want our church to eventually have a face-to-face relationship of people to people. Then people to pastor/leaders. That's one of the reasons we go out to teach in our house churches and international conferences.

"To be commissioned as a House of Zion after conferring with the Director of our Houses of Zion, they must come to Texas, learn from our team here, and then be commissioned. That way, we get to know them, as well as they get to know us, and then we have established a relationship with them. We have a five-page questionnaire that gives us good insight into who they are as a church and how they operate.

"Now, many members of our house churches might attend a regular local street church, but they are not getting from that church all that they need; so they also connect with us as well as continue to attend their local street church. I never discourage anyone from finding and attending a local street church in their locality. But in our house churches they are being moved in the *prophetic*. They begin to pray for the sick, they begin to expect miracles, and they begin to live an anointed life."

MINISTRIES OF ZION

"Next we have Ministries of Zion. These are people who have 501(c)3 ministries or organizations that have their own existence apart from Glory of Zion. But they align with us to be aligned apostolically. That gives them power and anointing for their ministry. I call this a 'functional covering.'

"People in ministries are committed to staying involved in their ministries. But one of our *apostolic* pastors becomes involved with them. Eventually they come to Texas to be commissioned for service."

BUSINESSES OF ZION

"We have another outreach called Businesses of Zion. We have our Zebulun School where people from all types of businesses are trained in the *prophetic* and *apostolic*. We have over 300 businesses aligned with Glory of Zion. There are people working forty hours a week (usually they own their business) making a living, but they want to have God's blessing on their business. They want *apostolic* covering over their business, so they align as a Business of Zion. Obviously, they are involved with the Sunday ministry as well as attending the schools."

CHURCHES OF ZION

"Finally, we have Churches of Zion. Consisting of 50 or more members, these are resident churches (i.e., street churches) that have already been established, but they realize something is missing in their ministries. They want more of God's blessing in their life and ministry. They want a covering, i.e., an *apostolic* authority. They may be 501(c)3 churches that may be recognized by the U.S. government and/or they may be local organized churches that have their own membership, buildings, services, etc. These are not house churches but operate through an actual church structure and usually own their own property and building. Some of these churches stream our entire worship services for their worship services, so that they join to worship live with us as we worship God. Some only stream the message. Of course, their people are individually worshiping in their location as are we in Texas. There are more than 500 churches that have aligned with Glory of Zion. Some of these are small, and some are large."

WORLDWIDE CONFERENCES

"We have conferences all over the world. Recently in Ecuador we rented a convention center and had over 300 leaders show up to be involved through an online connection to a conference being held in Corinth, Texas. The one difference is that they had their own (Spanish) worship in Ecuador, which was done separately from the worship in Texas. However, the ministry of the Word was streamed to them online so that everyone was together for the teaching. Distance does not limit the reach of Holy Spirit, and we saw the same anointing fall in Ecuador that was falling in Texas at the Global Spheres Center.

"We also have special events. Recently, I led a 100-day prayer focus where over 48,000 people signed up to pray with us. These are our *Zion-Aligned* individuals. They log in daily, hear from us about the power of prayer, and receive our emails telling them what God is doing for us.

"We have an astonishing amount of response from people in tithes and offerings. I don't count how much money comes in weekly, only monthly. We receive approximately $500,000 a month ($6 million a year)."

STRENGTH IN TEACHING

The success of every movement of God—or denomination—is tied to their commitment to its unique/central teaching of doctrine. While Presbyterianism/Calvinism is tied to God's sovereignty and His predestination, the strength of Chuck Pierce and Glory of Zion is its apostolic prophetic ministry with deep theological roots in both Israel and the church. Glory of Zion has aligned Jew and Gentile around Jesus Christ. Pierce is known for prophetic teaching directed at individuals, churches, cities, and nations. He claims, "If you understand the times and season in which we live, you can better prepare for the future."

Pierce believes in the fundamentals of the Christian faith and aligns himself with the doctrines of the Reformation. His teaching on God's covenant plan and promise to Abraham, including the land, children, and prosperity, has a unique impact for today.

God originally determined the boundaries of Israel, and changed the name of Abraham's grandson, Jacob, to Israel. That is the name of the land. Each of the twelve sons of Jacob were a part of the whole land of Israel, and when we Christians or our church or nation bless Israel, we receive the covenant blessings of the original promise to Abraham. Chuck teaches that each tribe of Israel has a redemptive blessing, and to understand it is to open oneself up to the blessing.

When God brought His people out of slavery in Egypt, He began leading them through the wilderness to the Promised Land. Chuck teaches that God brought each of the twelve tribes out as a warring army, with redemptive gifts. Without each tribe warring for their portion, the full plan of God for the land, called Israel, could not be fully manifested in the earth.

He teaches that of the twelve tribes, three tribes moved together. Judah, the apostolic leadership tribe, moved first. Next, Issachar, the Torah tribe. Issachar's blessing was that they understood times and could interpret the Word of God according to times (see 1 Chron. 12:32). The third tribe was Zebulun.

Chuck emphasizes that Jesus, Yeshua the Messiah, was born in the tribe of Judah and is the source to the fullness of God the Father's plan to redeem the lost. Jesus "became the Passover Lamb" to bring all mankind out of slavery and death. When Israel rejected Jesus as their Savior, He turned His heart toward the Gentiles. They are grafted into His glorious covenant that the

Father made with Abraham. His plan—the new covenant—allowed the redemptive qualities of each tribe to come alive in the church. This will allow the church to see God's plan for Israel fulfilled, and God's glory will cover the whole earth.

Pierce teaches that when "Gentiles receive grace and power to become sons of God through Christ, Israel will become jealous and turn toward their Messiah."

According to Pierce, "All nations on earth can become His inheritance. The time has come to harvest the nations and develop one new person in Jesus Christ, Jew and Gentile, as one."

So, what does that do to believers today? Pierce says, "God wants us to understand and interpret our times so we can prosper in everything and have wisdom to advance in all things." He goes on, "God is above time, but because of His love, He reaches down to intervene in time. He wants all people to see time from God's perspective and how His cycles are operating."

Chuck even says, "The unsaved see time as an endless repeated cycle that has no destination in the future. There is the hopelessness of the future, being linear, with no clear beginning and end. But God is moving history to a clear destination." In the process, Pierce sees some cycles drawing the church closer to Him in service and worship.

Pierce teaches that when a person comes into an understanding of God's times and seasons, they can break into His cycles of blessing. Many Christians don't know God's calendar. This timetable was revealed in the Old Testament and followed by the Jews and the apostles in the early church. But during the Dark Ages, the church turned from God's calendar to adopt the pagan Roman calendar. As a result, Christians lost the blessings of heaven that God wanted to pour out on them.

The message of hope is that "God is restoring His appointed times."

Pierce teaches that as believers, "You are free to celebrate God's seasons, or not, but when you choose to align your life with His appointed times, you enter into a cycle of blessing. God's cycle of harvest blessings of the Old Testament is available today. Once we understand the cycles of time, we go from increase to increase."

He teaches, "You have an inheritance. God is giving to each an incredible inheritance of blessing that He has prepared for all those who know Him and follow Him.

"God is not calling Christians to be Jews. But He does want believers to receive the blessings originally prepared for the Jews. True Christianity is the kind that the apostles knew. The blessings that they had in this glorious covenant are now available with all its promises and blessings of God's covenant with Abraham."

Christians are called to triumph over the enemy, i.e., the works of satan. God has raised up in every generation a people who are willing to war. The issue is to define the war and help people stay focused until they reach spiritual victory in Christ. This strategy is laid out in Pierce's books *The Future War of the Church* and *God's Unfolding Battle Plan*.

Chuck invites all who follow him to experience victory. When Jesus ascended to heaven, He sent the Holy Spirit to earth, and He indwells every believer. The Holy Spirit is the restraining force against the enemy. It is Pierce's duty to teach how to live for Christ and be an agent for the healing of the nations. The Holy Spirit points us to Jesus and gives us power to serve Him. His prayer for you: "Ask the Lord to experience the Holy Spirit today, just as in the day of Pentecost, only in a greater measure."

Chapter 8

NEW LIFE ASSEMBLY OF GOD

Chennai, South India
David Mohan, Pastor

The New Life Assembly of God, Chennai, South India (previously known as Madras), is the largest attended church in India (in the fourth largest city, population 8 million) with an average of 50,000 worshipers weekly in 5 campuses. They have planted 150 churches and send out missionaries around the world. Rev. David Mohan has turned the harvest field into a harvest force.

I arrived at the seven-story New Life Assembly of God before 5:00 in the morning June 2016. The swarm of people walking to the church overwhelmed me...it was dark outside and over 5,000 were walking to church. The church only had about three dozen parking places. At first I thought I was assigned the early morning time because the visiting pastors with me got the best times later in the morning. However, I was honored with the choice of 5:00 AM because I was the oldest (age 85 at the time), and because the biggest crowds came early—it was only 85 degrees at that time of day; the temperatures would reach over 100 by 11:00 AM.

The large auditorium for the Tamil language service was on the first floor (I preached through an interpreter), and the English service was on the second floor (I preached there at 11:00 AM). Today, the church has six services in Tamil (auditorium seats 4,500), five services in English (auditorium seats 1,300), and three services in other languages. Interestingly, the Tamil speakers mostly walk to church, while the English-speaking crowd drive because they live a distance from the church.

EARLY BEGINNINGS

India is the birthplace of four world religions—Hinduism, Jainism, Buddhism, Sikhism—and has the second-largest Muslim population in the world. Yet Christianity is not only surviving, Pentecostalism is the fastest-growing Protestant group in this country according to Pew Research.

David Mohan began the church in a small rented house in a single room with seven people. The room could hold only 15 people. The homeowner changed his mind about having a church meet in his facilities. They came one Sunday to find the two rooms filled with bags of cement. Mohan knew he had to find another meeting place. He found a vacant plot of ground and built a "shelter" with a thatched roof for shade from the sun and protection from the rain. The church grew to six hundred.

A hurricane destroyed the thatched shelter and the men of the church had to rebuild it. Then the owner of the plot of ground wouldn't let them use the land. The church used a YMCA gym when there was not a game scheduled. The church prayed from 9:00 PM till midnight for a new building. In addition, Mohan prayed from 5:00 to 8:00 each morning. He feels prayer is the only answer because the nation of India has been "steeped" in demonism for decades.

God told Mohan, "Now is the time to stop praying and start praising." The pastor said he didn't know where the church would be, but he knew it would be on a main road to attract attenders. As he praised God for a new location, God was stretching his faith.

A family agreed to sell the church a plot of land on Mount Road. The church constructed another thatched roof shelter for seven hundred. The church continued growing and began multiple services. Still they didn't have much money to build, but they kept sending offerings to overseas missions. Mohan felt it was necessary to have a "giving" church for missions, not just collect money for their church needs. "Soul winning is important all over the world, not just at home."

After two years, a spark from a sawmill next to the church caught the thatched roof on fire, destroying everything. For nine months they again met in the YMCA while they erected a new structure, this time with a roof that would not burn so easily.

The church continued growing. Two years after the fire, it rained ten straight days. The walls of the new church crumbled. Mohan cried out, "Why? Why is my church destroyed over and over again?" The Lord spoke to him that other churches that were not growing didn't have problems, but the enemy persecutes his church because they are winning souls. Then Mohan realized, "My calling is to build strong souls for the kingdom of God that fire or flood cannot destroy."

PRAYER MINISTRY

David was asked how he built one of the largest churches in India. "We have always put a lot of effort into praying. Because by prayer and faith, the Holy Spirit moves among us and did this wonderful work."

Mohan credits early growth to approximately 50 prayer cells that prayed for people who were being won to Christ. Mohan said, "If I want my church to be a praying church, I must first be praying." He joins the prayer ministry each morning at 5:00 AM for three hours of prayer. Then he added, "I go away from the city for ten days of prayer and fasting each year." There he is asking for God's vision, goals, and themes for the coming year.

The ladies have a prayer ministry from 10:00 AM until noon each day. The men have a prayer ministry from 9:00 AM to 11:00 AM each Saturday. Twice a year the pastoral staff spends two days in prayer and fasting for the church. The church has several other regular prayer events, involving around 12,000 to 15,000 people.

TURNING INDIA'S HARVEST FIELD INTO A HARVEST FORCE

Most churches in India reach about 50 to 60 souls relying on the pastor to be the spiritual leader who prays for members and visits them. But the Lord was showing Mohan a different way. The people are the church and they should pray for each other's healing and give godly counsel; they should be winning souls. He felt if he could get some to minister for Christ to others, his church could multiply and influence many lost people.

The cell-based model of discipleship was introduced in 1993, which grew out of groups of people gathering for prayer. Mohan said when the people understood the priesthood of all believers involved more than praying, those in the cell groups began to be discipled and equipped for outreach, adding to the growth.

David saw many people coming whom he did not know and could not remember their faces. He began looking for help to manage such a large number of people. He visited Singapore and met a pastor of small groups who explained how he could minister through small groups. Mohan invited the pastor to come to Chennai to help him. "One pastor can take care of 50 people, but when 200 come, one pastor can't take care of their spiritual need s. It is there, the people must be taught evangelism, nurture, and discipleship. Because leaders were trained in small groups, multitudes have continued to come to our churches."

Mohan testifies, "I knew how to teach and preach, but I didn't know how to administer a large church so each believer could be properly discipled." He began to read about the cell ministry of Yonggi Cho's large church in Korea. Through that ministry, he saw how all believers could minister to each other so no one was left behind. His church had home Bible studies in place, but there were "no goals, no structure, and no tools."

Mohan began to set goals for the people and for the small groups. First, training was provided for the "care groups" so that each group had a leader who was qualified with training. Next, each group was given evangelism goals to reach out to the unsaved. The purpose was to win souls that resulted in growing groups that could be multiplied.

The church previously had men and women's fellowship groups and youth groups, but people attended, listened, but were not challenged to flex their spiritual muscles and reach out to the others who needed the gospel. Now Mohan believes his main task is to train every believer to do ministry so the church multiplies.

How do they organize and guide outreach? Mohan has people in a group identify someone in their household or family they would like to see come to Christ. They plan a birthday party for the unbeliever to honor them and present salvation. Also, he urges cell members to invite unsaved friends or family to attend a worship service, then plan to get the person together with their small group. "We don't want the unsaved to think of us as a big church, but rather a small group where they are known by name and they get to know them individually." Mahan says, "Pastoral care can't come from me to each one of the thousands in the church. I give care to the leaders who then pass it on to all so that pastoral care comes from close friends and relatives who are in Christ."

When a care group grows, it is ready to multiply. The group is broken in two so each group continues to grow and multiply. If a group doesn't grow, leaders check on their progress, counsel with leaders, and help them get on the right track.

Mohan says, "Television evangelists and big evangelists have a part and place, but they cannot touch the common people."

But grass-roots evangelism—person to person—will touch the hearts and lives of the people and bring them to the church. He does not discount television evangelism and big crusades, but for real church growth, local people—who are local evangelists—must go out to speak to everyone. He emphasizes relationship, friendship, and bringing people to the church.

CHADWICK MOHAN

Pastor David Mohan preaches in the Tamil service; his son Chadwick supervises the English service, and usually preaches there. The church began using the Tamil language because it was the regional language, the one most spoken in Chennai. However, the city has seen explosive growth in both commercialism and industry, including professional and educated leaders whose primary language is English. This is because of the growth of the industrial IT and financial markets in the city. The English language section of the church is growing.

Today, Mohan is the main preacher in the Tamil service, and Chadwick preaches in the English service. How do they manage with two broad groups of people coming to the church? Initially, the English service was begun in 1999 with mostly young adults attending the English service and the older members who use the native language attending the preaching service of the older Mohan.

There were other adjustments. Chadwick introduced curriculum for the small group ministry. The church has seen growing strength in this addition, but even then there were difficulties. Those speaking Tamil lived closer to one another and could easily gather for small group meetings; however, the professionals attending the church lived farther from the church and their houses were widely scattered. It was difficult for them to get included in small group activities. However, the strength of interaction and fellowship overcame this difficulty.

There was another shift while the father oversaw the larger Tamil congregation. Chadwick put together a seven-member oversight team to coordinate ministry for the English-speaking members. Chadwick coached them, and he is quoted, "If we decide anything, we decide together. It is not 'my' decision, it's 'our' decision."

Chadwick has a Doctor of Ministry degree from Gordon Conwell Theological Seminary near Boston in the U.S., in addition to three other degrees, and is married with one son.

WRAP UP

Christianity represents only about two or three percent of the population in India. Mohan says, "We must pray for people who criticize us, and pray for people who persecute us. There has always been persecution of Christianity throughout history, but through persecution many people come to know Christ. We must not hate those who persecute us but love and pray for them and stand firm for our faith in Christ."

David Mohan is called the spiritual father of India; he is the General Superintendent of the Assemblies of God of India, chairman of the National Association of Evangelists, and chairman of the National Coalition of Unreached People.

Chennai (formally Madras) is the capital of the state Tamil Nadu, located near the Bay of Bengal near the Port of São Tomé (named after Saint Thomas who came to the area between 52 and 70 AD). The area is Hindu, but the oldest Christian church in India is the São Tomé Church believed to begun by the apostle Thomas, who also was martyred in the area. The Portuguese first arrived in 1522 and began building the port of São Tomé. The English East India Company bought land there in 1639. In the early years, missionaries from Scotland, the United Kingdom, and France were sent there. Therefore, Chennai has a rich Protestant tradition but is primarily a Hindu culture. There are many Protestant churches—8,000 Assembly of God churches in India—but New Life is the largest and most dominant.

THE FUTURE

The church purchased 30 acres of ground for expansion and future ministry. They plan to build a 55,000-seat stadium. The property was owned by 200 different individuals. Mohan thought he could never get that many to agree to sell to the church. But God worked miracles for it to happen. It will be the largest Assembly of God church building in the world. But to Mohan, a church of 55,000 is a tiny portion of 10 million people living in the area.

Construction of the 55,000-seat facility will take place in phases. First, a 6,000-seat tabernacle style auditorium will be built. The second phrase will include a training center and hostel. After that multiple expansions will take place until a 55,000-seat semi-amphitheater is completed. At the ground breaking in 2007, over 15,000 people watched the fireworks celebration and attended the laying of the cornerstone. Thomas E. Trask, General Superintendent of the Assemblies of God, spoke at the ceremony.

The church has sponsored planting 200 new Assembly of God churches in the state of Madras. One brother, Chris Doss, launched a new church 10 years ago and now has launched 11 more churches.

Mohan feels his church can plant 1,000 churches with one million believers trained in care groups. "I believe we can evangelize the entire Indian subcontinent." The new 55,000-seat stadium is the next step to complete that vision: "turning the harvest field into a harvest force."

Chapter 9

FAITH TO BUILD
a Church of 100,000 Worshipers

**The Word of Hope Church, Manila, Philippines
David Sobrepeña, Pastor**

David Sobrepeña, a financial consultant and investment broker in the United States, was called by God to move to the Philippians to plant a church that today averages over 60,000 worshipers in multi-campus churches and life groups (cell groups) meeting around the city. His church has over the years planted over 500 churches throughout the Philippine Islands. Sobrepeña's goal is 100,000 members.

The Word of Hope Church in the Philippines has over 60,000 worshipers assembling in multi-services throughout the islands and in its large auditorium in Manila that seats 6,500 across the street from SM City, the largest mall in the Philippines and the Pacific Rim. Word of Hope advertises itself as one of the largest churches of born-again believers in the Philippines, and pastor David Sobrepeña has a vision of reaching 100,000 in attendance in home groups (life groups) and planting new satellite churches on every island of the Philippines.

The church began in the heart of David Sobrepeña long before its first meeting in a theater in Manila. He was living in greater Dallas, Texas, working for Merrill-Lynch, a financial investment bank, and had everything that the American dream required—a custom home, three cars, a speedboat, and a retirement plan for the future.

One night he saw on the television footage of the revolution of the people in the Philippines against their government.

When David saw the revolution going on in the Philippines, he heard the Lord's voice say to him, "Why don't you go back?" He answered, "If You will be with me...I will do it." The call from God was so real and urgent; he had no other alternative.

God also spoke in a clear voice for him to go back and offer the people "a word of hope." God told him to build a church—a big one to give his people hope. That's where the church got its name.

"Lord, if that's what You want me to do, just provide for my needs," was Sobrepeña's prayer.

David Sobrepeña was born in the Philippines, but had come to America with a plan to settle down in America. Now God has called him back home.

David applied to the foreign missions department of the Assemblies of God, his denomination, and waited one year for a reply. They wrote that his resume didn't qualify him for mission service, and beyond that the mission didn't send people back to their own country. But according to David, the letter released him from an obligation to go to the Philippines. He prayed, "Thank You, God, I'm off the hook." But God had other plans that included a tour of the Philippines to survey the possibilities.

David sold one of his family cars to finance a missionary trip to the Philippines. He took a leave of absence from his job. He only wanted to find out what God had for him in the Philippines. He preached in youth camps and evangelistic crusades, continually asking God, "If it is Your will for me to stay here, speak to me now, or I'll go back to Dallas, never to return to the Philippines."

To his surprise God said to him, "I want you to go to SM City, but SM City is not really a city; it is the largest mall in the Philippines." David visited the management of the mall asking about renting the facilities to start Bible studies. They indicated they didn't rent facilities for religious activities, but the manager directed him across the street. "Why don't you rent the Paramount Theater across the street?" It was the busiest highway in all the Philippines.

David knew the theater well. It's along EDSA, the place where the revolution began that threw Ferdinand Marcos out of government. In the providence of God that's where the church is located.

David scheduled a meeting with the owner of the Paramount Theater and couldn't believe he was saying, "I want to rent your theater for a church." The owner thought he had thousands of members, so he entered into serious negotiations. The owner suggested, "Come back and give me a real estate proposal and I will entertain it."

David understood how to write a real estate proposal from his brokerage business, so the next day he returned, "Here is my lease agreement with an option to buy."

The owner read it quickly, liked it, and said, "I'll have my lawyers study it and get back to you in seven days."

David had one prayer request, "God, if it is Your will for me to come back to the Philippines to start a church, this man must rent us the theater."

He had been told the owner said, "No," to everyone. So, David was surprised when seven days later he received the contract back, which was modified by the lawyers. And the owner said, "Here's the contract...sign it."

Sobrepeña's knees began to shake; he had run out of money for his trip to the Philippines. He had not yet told his wife, Nellie, of his plans to move back to the Philippines. So, he began to pray, "God, if this is Your will, speak to my wife, Nellie, to approve everything." If ever a leader took a leap of faith in the dark, this was *brinkmanship faith*.

When he arrived back in the United States, he invited his wife to an expensive Chinese restaurant in downtown Dallas. There he shared with her what God had done through his preaching crusades in the Philippines. He described many souls were saved, but he didn't say anything about renting the Paramount Theater.

The next day he took her to the most expensive Japanese restaurant, and here he again talked about their commitment to God before they were married. They had promised to serve God wherever He called them.

The following day he took her to dinner to the most expensive and classy steak house in Arlington, Texas. While they were getting seated, she asked, "What are you doing? We've never gone out to dinner three times in a row. You're leading up to something."

It took five weeks for Nellie to agree to sell everything and move to the Philippines.

David visited Republic National Bank to tell them he wanted to turn his mortgage back to them, forgetting about the equity. They tried to get him to sell the house and then pay off the loan, but he said, "I don't have time to wait...God has called me to the Philippines."

The manager from the bank gave him the paperwork and he signed it. The house was gone. In the next few weeks they began selling off personal property. They had an auction at the First Assembly of God, Irving, Texas, where most of their personal property was sold through auction. Some of the hardest things for David to sell were his hunting rifle and fishing rods. This was evidence of *sacrificial faith*.

David and his wife went to their folks in Seattle, Washington, left their two youngest children temporarily, and with their eldest son flew to Manila. They did not know what was ahead, but God was leading them.

They rented a small room to save what funds they had left. The following day David paid a down payment on the theater to the owner and took possession.

People thought David was crazy for starting a church in such a large theater. When pastors want to plant a church, they usually begin a church in a small house, an office space, or under a coconut tree—not the largest theater with 1,400 seats in Manila.

But David felt God had called him, so he trusted God to build a big church. "If God is not in it, I would pack my bags and go back to the United States and start all over again."

He advertised on three radio stations five to seven times a day for the next three weeks. He printed tens of thousands of fliers to be distributed around the mall and in a neighborhood area.

David got 17 volunteers from a local Bible college. They began a Jericho march claiming victory around the inside of the theater. Then they anointed each seat and asked God to save people who would sit in that seat. They had to re-wire the auditorium and had to make sure there was enough light—movie theaters are known for their darkness.

One hundred fifty people showed up on opening day. David preached his best sermon on Calvary. He had prayed, "If no one comes forward for salvation, I will pack my bags and go home."

But more than 20 people came forward that first day; among them was the entire Tabudlong family. Today the Tabudlong parents are now passed away, but their daughter Donna is a children's pastor for the church, and her brother is one of the key leaders in their men's ministry.

David Sobrepeña's greatest surprise in life is how God took him—he wanted to stay out of ministry—and thrust him into one of the most effective ministries in Asia. David's grandfather was a minister, his father was a minister; all he wanted to do was stay away from the ministry. He testified, "Although I believed that God could do tremendous things...it's beyond belief that God could use me to plant and grow a church."

Even when David went back to the Philippines, he expected God to build a huge church for him—2,000 or 3,000 people—not a super church of over 60,000 people.

Within the first year of the church, God brought in over 2,000 people under its pastoral care. The church was recognized as the fastest growing church in the Philippines; its total income was about $5,000 per month. That's outstanding considering the average worker was receiving about $3.00 a day and the church was surrounded by slums on one side and a very big shopping mall on the other.

Finally, there came a time when the owner of the theater notified David that the church had to vacate the premises. He began looking for places to move the church, but there was nothing big enough to hold that many people. Also, cost was an issue. He continued to pray. God kept telling him, "Trust Me." When the leaders of the church came together with David to pray, God showed them a piece of property one block away from the theatre. Again, right across the street from the largest mall in Asia. The vacant lot was for sale. They prayed that God would give them the property and decided to make an offer, although they didn't have the money.

David made an appointment to talk with the owners of the property; it cost $1 million for less than an acre. They agreed on a price and the owner said, "I will give you a contract if you will write me a check for $50,000 as down payment, 48 postdated checks for $25,000 for each month thereafter"—48 months of postdated financial obligations.

David agreed to the terms and borrowed $50,000 for the down payment for the property. Then he gave the owner a checkbook with 48 post-dated checks, each one $25,000 for the next four years. Again, this was *brinkmanship faith*. He was taking a leap into the unknown, expecting God to provide.

At the time, the church was only receiving around $7,000 a month in income. David reminds that in the Philippines it is not against the law to write a "hot" post-dated check, while it is against the law in the United States. He had no other option but do it.

David knew that if the money were not there, it was against the Filipino law to deposit a post-dated check when there were not sufficient funds to cover it. He would be sued and could go to jail if the check bounced.

The church began building on the property immediately. And David appealed to the people to give all they could, but that still was not enough to pay the seller for the steel, building supplies, and concrete. In addition to all of that, if he didn't pay the seller/developer, all the improvements would revert to the seller.

David stood before his people to tell them they needed an offering of $75,000 the next Sunday. This was miracle Sunday.

They only received $10,000, and thought that they had done all they could, even though it was much larger than the $2,500 weekly offerings they had been receiving.

David went home, fell on his face, and began crying unto God. He kept telling the Lord, "Not only will I not finish the building, I will lose everything."

David phoned the corporation that sold him the piece of ground. He asked to speak to the chairman of the board, but he was not available. The following day the chairman called back to say, "Reverend, what is it you need?" He explained to the owner his financial predicament and asked him to hold the checks for the next three months, because he couldn't pay for them until the building was completed.

The owner said he couldn't do that because it was against the policy of the board, but he would dismiss the four percent penalty.

The following day the chairman of the board had a courier deliver a letter personally to David. When he opened it, there were three personal checks from him covering the mortgage for the next three months. David said, "It was a miracle!"

DEFINE FAITH

When David was asked to define faith he said, "Faith is walking on water." He explained it as doing something you cannot do naturally, and you don't expect to do. "Faith is doing God's work when there is no visible means for financial support, and there is no way you can honestly get the job done...you just do it.

"Walking by faith is walking like Peter walked. When Jesus said 'come,' Peter stepped out of the boat and believed the word of Jesus.

"The key for me is to do the work of Jesus by obeying the word of Jesus. People criticize me for the way I do ministry, but I just do what Jesus tells us in His Word to do. Then when I pray, He tells me what to do and I do it. Faith is really obeying Jesus' words, and it looks like walking on water."

In 2017 they have acquired over 50,000 new decisions for Christ through church services, evangelistic crusades (through their gospel boat and gospel bus), and medical missions. In 2018, they led over 100,000 people to make decisions for Christ. David is seeking God for 125,000 decisions in 2019.

David began life groups in 2014. Today the church has 8,700 life groups. These follow the example of David Yonggi Cho, pastor of Full Gospel Church, Seoul, South Korea. The church in Korea had at one time 35,000 groups meeting in homes, restaurants, apartments, exercise rooms, etc. Sobrepeña's goal is to have 10,000 life groups by 2020.

In addition, the church has a total of nine Sunday preaching services and 47 campuses (multisite ministries). That gives the church over 50,000 in weekly attendance.

Word of Hope plans to plant 35 new satellite churches in Metro Manila and will reach 100,000 members by the year 2025.

Through the leadership of David Sobrepeña the church has established the Hope General Hospital, Hope Christian Academy, Hope Leadership College, and Paradise Prayer Garden (a venue for retreats, summer camps, weddings, sports, and recreation). Also, he has established Hope Inc., a micro-finance enterprise that will help empower the urban poor through jobs and livelihood opportunities.

As a result of his passion to reach lost people a few years ago, the church purchased its first gospel boat, a 100-foot power yacht that carries the gospel team from one island to another in the Philippines. They dock and hold evangelistic crusades. Today, the church has two gospel boats.

In the same way, the church purchased its first gospel bus to travel to hold evangelistic crusades in schools, market places, open streets, and open-air plazas, all with the view of planting a gospel preaching church. Now it has two gospel buses and a kids' mobile as well as a kids' customized truck for children evangelism.

The purpose of all the preaching services, including the gospel services held in the two gospel boats and the two gospel buses, is to evangelize and plant new churches. But both the gospel buses and gospel boats offer medical missions and, through Operation Hope (a relief operation), distribute food and clothing to the masses. But more than humanitarian ministry, the passion is always to begin new churches.

David Sobrepeña has been used greatly to spread the gospel in the Philippines but has also had a ministry in many other countries of the world. He has travelled to all the six continents except Antarctica to speak in Christian leadership and church conferences and open-air crusades, and he is recognized as a world leader.

Sobrepeña has worked with John Maxwell's EQUIP organization, working not only in the Philippines but also in the Asia Pacific Region. He is a member of the EQUIP leadership hall of fame, as well as working with many other Christian organizations throughout the Philippines.

He is presently the national president and general superintendent of the Assemblies of God in the Philippines and has served as chairman of the Philippine Council of Evangelical Churches and has served on the Board of the Philippine Bible Society.

David and Nellie Sobrepeña have three grown-up children and are happy with their five grandchildren.

Chapter 10

TRANSLATING SCRIPTURES
to Plant 40,000 House Churches and 5,000 Street Churches

Love Fellowship
Southern Asia
Dr. Raj[1]

By faith Dr. Raj has planted 40,000 house churches and 5,000 street churches. He sends church planters to unreached villages to pray over the town and prayer walk through the town to prepare the areas for evangelism. This church planter is also called a man of peace who shares the gospel as he plants house churches. He mobilizes and teaches the people to translate the Bible from a trade language into the language of the town and area. Already 46 languages have a New Testament. By faith, Raj has innovated and perfected the Church Centric Bible Translation Philosophy (CCBT).

Dr. Raj was born and raised in an orthodox Syrian Christian church to born-again parents. At the young age of 15 he received Jesus. When he was 17 years old, he was baptized and joined a Pentecostal church.

While in medical school, the Lord challenged him to become a missionary. After graduation, during his tenure as a medical doctor, he began evangelizing and at the age of 24 established his first church.

In 1988, the Holy Spirit burdened him about lost souls, and he shared his burden with some friends. They started a prayer movement that gradually developed momentum resulting in the formation of Love Fellowship. For the next 11 years he coordinated the prayer ministry while serving as a physician. In 1999, the Lord clearly guided him to leave secular engagements and concentrate fully on the prayer vision. Since then he continues as a consulting physician.

Love Fellowship[2] is a network of churches and missions that carry out the Great Commission task in South Asia. Thirty years ago, it began as a prayer movement focusing on four areas: 1) establishing communities of believers (churches), 2) equipping indigenous leaders, 3) empowering the poor, and 4) engaging the scripture-less with the Word of God.

Since their inception, this network has planted around 5,000 regular Sunday churches (called street churches because they have a location) and 50,000 house churches in South Asia. One of their major initiatives is scripture translation into the native languages of the people using Church Centric Bible Translation Methodology (https://www.ccbt.bible). They use a Bible that is already translated into the Hindi trade languages as the source text. Translation is done by volunteers in the new church assisted by technology tools and translation specialists. Dr. Raj says, "We have a responsibility to the multitudes of our nation that do not have a Bible in their language, and that's why we translate the scriptures into their heart languages." There are 738 languages in India of which more than 500 are still waiting to receive the first copy of the scriptures in their native language.

The Church Based Bible Translation (CCBT) project is the biggest step of faith he has taken. There was no precedent, no literature to guide him, or any personnel who could tell him what to do.

Many discouraged him, even questioning the viability of the project. But this step of faith has seen abundant results and is growing. Now there are resource people, volunteers, dedicated staff, training facilities and technological know-how.

In the fall of 2017, they dedicated the New Testament in 12 Bible-less languages for the first time. Over 600 church leaders attended this dedication service and I was there to witness this "God moment." This movement has now become a new paradigm in Bible translation and is now recognized globally as a faster, cheaper, and better method of scripture translation. Since then, this movement has released 34 additional New Testaments and is currently working on many more languages including 38 Old Testament translations. Availability of scriptures in every language not only accelerates church planting, but it also helps the church to become healthy and rooted in God's Word.

> "Our desire is to have New Testaments in every language of our nation by 2025 and a full Bible by 2030."

CHURCH CENTRIC
BIBLE TRANSLATION MOVEMENT

In the fall of 2017, at the conference held by Love Fellowship, 12 New Testaments were dedicated and presented to the team who were involved in the translation process. These 12 translation teams representing 12 different languages until then did not have a copy of the scriptures in their language.

The strategy of translating the Bible into a foreign language has radically changed since the first missionary did it. Previously biblical scholars would spend years and years translating and perfecting a copy of the scriptures. William Carey, the first missionary to India, translated the Bible in an Indian language. It took 25 years to produce it and then another five years correcting and polishing his work.

The new strategy is "bottom-up." Churches driving the translation process use average Christian believers assisted by trained mother-tongue translators and quality checkers who are theologically trained and proficient in both the native and their trade languages. Some teams will write pages after pages, while others directly edit using drafting tools. The teams then go back over to proofread, correct, and polish it to make it as accurate as they can. All final translations are checked by trained consultants.

They do not translate from the Greek or Hebrew; rather, they read a Bible that is already available in their trade language and then translate it into the local ethnic language.

In contrast to the copyright restrictions of popular Bible translation agencies, Dr. Raj believes that all scriptures should be freely available to the community for distribution and further modification, checking, and feedback thus increasing the quality of the translations. CCBT removes the copyright issues and increases the availability of resources thus naming it as "The free Bible translation movement." "Freely you have received, freely give" (Matt. 10:8).

But more than a Bible translation endeavor, it is all about planting and establishing strong and healthy churches; it is all about finishing the Great Commission task by reaching every language group (see Rev. 7:9). As soon as a portion of the scriptures is translated, the church planters distribute it to believers and to their family members so they can share the excitement of reading God's Word in their own heart language. They not only distribute printed Bibles but also audio Bibles so that even illiterate people can listen to God's Word. This powerful tool motivates curiosity to know what is in the Bible and to read or listen to something in their own language.

In recent years, several Bible translation agencies have improved their strategy so that a New Testament can be produced in ten years. However, the "bottom-up" strategy used by Love Fellowship produces a New Testament in two years.

I was present to dedicate twelve New Testaments that had been translated into a native language that previously did not have the scriptures. There were approximately 100 printed copies of each language on a small table on the platform at Love Fellowship. Approximately 7 to 17 members of each translating team came to the platform when their New Testament was formally presented and dedicated in prayer. They stood and "laid hands" on the newly printed copies of the New Testament. They represented professional men and women, Christian leaders, secular educators, lawyers, and business leaders. Most were university graduates and some donated their time as a humanitarian project. But in the process they became Christians as they interacted with the Word of

God. Jesus is also called the Word (see John 1:1,14). They came to know Him personally as they studied the "words" of Scripture, where they found eternal life (see John 6:68-69).

There has been a total of 46 languages that have been translated into the New Testament through the ministry of Love Fellowship in the past two years.

TWO PARADIGMS OF BIBLE TRANSLATION

Pattern One

The traditional strategy adopted by the majority of the Bible translation agencies in the world adhere to a translation strategy often referred to as Paradigm One. In a typical scenario a Western missionary goes to a third-world country (like Nigeria or Nepal), identifies a village or culture or tribe, learns the language, and assimilates the culture of the people. He/she then breaks down their spoken language into a written expression of words, symbols, and grammar. The new translation must make sense to those who speak this heart language in that culture. Then grammar is written in their language that comes out of the work of translating. Finally, the missionary must translate the Scriptures into the native language. Normally it takes about 25 years and the average cost of production for a New Testament is about $200 per verse.

Pattern Two

Approximately 25 years ago another strategy was developed to translate the scriptures. One group using this strategy,

The Seed Company in Arlington, Texas, said that the traditional approach takes too much time and money. They began by getting mother-tongue translators (a converted person from that language group) to translate the Bible. This person was not usually a trained minister or a trained scholar. This translator knows the Bible and loves it, and from that passion translates the scriptures into his/her tongue. The Seed Company approach translates the Bible based on sight and understanding of the text. The strategy to get the scripture translated using mother-tongue translators is referred to as Paradigm Two. However, this methodology is also controlled by translation consultants who are often Westerners who will have to check every verse using a "back-translation" to examine the accuracy of the translation. The church will have to wait till it is perfected by the consultant and published. This new pattern reduced the translation time of the New Testament from 25 years to 10 years, and the cost from $200 to $50 per verse.

But even with this phenomenal breakthrough, the unfinished task of Bible translation is still huge. There are 7,111 languages in the world (https://www.ethnologue.com), but only 683 languages have a whole Bible and 1,534 languages have got the New Testament (http://www.wycliffe.net/en/statistics). Nearly 1.5 billion people out of the seven billion people in the world still do not have a full Bible and another 800 million still do not have a New Testament in their heart language. This is what calls for a new paradigm.

The new approach developed by Dr. Raj, and followed by many others, is called *Paradigm X Bible Translation Movement.* He believes that completing the task of translating the Bible in every language can only be accomplished using a new Paradigm. Because he did not know what it would take, he named it Paradigm X. Churches are being planted throughout the world among various tribes, people groups, or ethnic groups that have no written languages. Many of the people are illiterate. This is also described as the oral culture. Beyond that, many cannot read beyond the introductory level. They are called pre-oral. This calls for not only the availability of printed scriptures but also audio translations and perhaps many remaining languages may only need oral translations.

Many are using storytelling as an evangelistic tool. Those who cannot read or write also do not think in logical sequences of ideas, but they think simply in images or pictures or sequences of events. They can be reached better by telling the stories of the Bible rather than trying to use a logical presentation of the gospel.

Today because of the aggressive mobilization campaigns, 1) the Bible is being translated by the people doing evangelism; 2) their translation is owned by the new church community and not by a mission board, translation agency, or a Bible society; and 3) this new paradigm is technology-assisted because advanced IT technology is now available to all, so even the newest church has enough technology to guide the Bible translation. Also, new technology will give quality assurance, translating from a scripture that is accurate and using translation resources available in their gateway languages. These new translations will be free to distribute. There are no copyright issues, nor must a fee be paid to an agency.

This New Approach Will Be

1. church-based
2. community-owned
3. technologically-assisted
4. quality-assured, and

5. a free translation movement

Dr. Raj is part of a global Church Centric Bible Translation forum (CCBT) and Every Tribe Every Nation (ETEN) movement. Their goal is that 95 percent of the people in the world should have access to the full Bible, 99.9 percent of the people must have a New Testament, and 100 percent of the people in the world must have at least 25 chapters of the Bible in their heart language by 2033.

The passion of Dr. Raj is to get the whole Bible translated into every language of South Asia by 2030. The first step is to start with the New Testament, then add Psalms, Proverbs, and then the whole Bible. This is also supplemented by Bible stories and other discipleship tools in their language.

Eighty percent of pastors in South Asia do not have any theological education. They are laymen who have been trained in their churches to go out to plant churches. In the CCBT movement, the local lingual church community is responsible for the translation assisted by a team of trained mother-tongue translators and quality checkers. They believe in an iterative improvement in quality as the church digs deeper into the scriptures as part of the discipleship process.

STARFISH CHURCH PLANTING

"Church planting is like a starfish producing more starfish," explains Dr. Raj. "This approach explains why we have been successful in planting new churches.

"When you first see a starfish, you realize it has five sections like a star. Even though it is a brittle invertebrate, if a starfish is cut into five pieces, it becomes five starfishes; and each new section can become a full starfish. In other words, every section of the starfish has potential for multiplication.

"Compare that with an octopus. If you cut an arm off an octopus, what will happen? The arm will die. The octopus will not have the use of that arm for the rest of its life.

"These represent two kinds of churches. A starfish church has the potential for multiplication because every believer has been discipled and trained and has the potential for multiplication. When one or more believers are separated from their church, they have the potential of reproducing themselves in another believer or reproducing themselves in another church."

But an octopus church is an illustration of a dead or dying church. When an arm is cut off, it dies. When a member is disassociated with their church, they usually die. They do not have the vitality or vision of beginning a new church and the church is not able to replace it either.

In the New Testament, when believers were persecuted in one place (see Acts 8:1-4), they went elsewhere planting churches (see Acts 11:19). They were like the starfish because they reproduced themselves. They were not like the octopus.

In a starfish church, every believer has the potential of starting a church. In Acts 8, persecution breaks out in the early church. "Now Saul was consenting to his death. At that time a great persecution arose against the church which was at Jerusalem; and they were all scattered throughout the regions of Judea and Samaria, except the apostles.... Therefore those who were scattered went everywhere preaching the word" (Acts 8:1,4). Where did these persecuted Christians go? Some went to Antioch and some went elsewhere: "Now those who were scattered after the persecution that arose over Stephen traveled as far as Phoenicia, Cyprus, and Antioch, preaching the word to no one but the Jews only" (Acts 11:19). What did they do? They began an assembly and "a great number believed and turned to the Lord" (Acts 11:21). The word *added* is technically implying a list or roll of a church. "Many people were added to the Lord" (Acts 11:24). The net result was that several churches were planted in the region, including the church at Antioch.

CHURCH PLANTING BY THE MAN OF PEACE

Church planting begins when a single person or two people as a team go to a village to plant a church. They begin praying before they get to the village. When they arrive, they *prayer walk* to prepare the ground for the sowing of the seed of the gospel. While they are prayer walking, they look for a *man of peace* in that town. They follow the pattern suggested by Jesus.

> *After these things the Lord appointed seventy others also, and sent them two by two before His face into every city and place..."But whatever house you enter, first say, 'Peace to this house.' And if a son of peace is there, your peace will rest on it; if not, it will return to you. And remain in the same house...Do not go from house to house...And heal the sick there, and say to them, 'The kingdom of God has come near to you'"* (Luke 10:1-9).

Westerners want to evangelize or plant a church by distributing literature, conducting mass crusades, and various other means. Dr. Raj teaches church planting by staying in the home of the man of peace, winning him to Christ, and beginning gospel services in his home. If he is truly saved, he will share his faith with his extended family (*oikos*) including friends, relatives, associates, and neighbors, and slowly the church in his house begins to grow.

He teaches prayer walking so people see you praying.[3] When they ask what you are doing, give them the message of salvation. The one who is interested will listen to you; he will invite you to the hospitality of his home—he is the man of peace. When the man of peace is discipled and becomes strong, he will share his faith with his friends, family, associates, and neighbors (these are the extended family he will bring into his house church) and slowly one new church is planted.

Dr. Raj teaches early intentional discipleship of new believers in each church. Every believer must be taught the Great Commission and how to witness to what Jesus Christ has done in their life as soon as they are saved. Once they start sharing their faith with their friends, family, associates, and neighbors, the church starts growing.

Slowly some believers will get a vision to start a similar house church in their own home. They will open their own homes for "house churches."

Unless properly trained, new church planters would not be able to plant churches and will face changes and fail in their ministry. Do not follow Western methods of church planting in a culture that is not Western. In villages of South Asia, as well as other non-Western villages, often evangelistic techniques used in the West may not work. Mass evangelism strategies have often been less effective in pioneer fields in South Asia, while a simple approach like the *man of peace* strategy will work better.

Dr. Raj through the Love Fellowship continues to actively encourage newly planted churches to align themselves with the "starfish" model of church multiplication to help them carryout the goal of reaching their people groups, as well as other unevangelized groups.

Love Fellowship is not an organization that controls or keeps its churches but rather encourages them to be strong, healthy, and multiplying, while remaining faithful through the proper interpretation of the scriptures. This calls for training of the leaders of the emerging churches, but they cannot get theological education from a seminary or a Bible college. A majority of these effective church planters are not educated enough to enter a theological education program. However, they are the real people who need theological training because their influence is widespread among the local communities of believers. So Dr. Raj believes in theological education for all using church-based theological education. He is also involved in South Asia Forum for Non Formal Theological Education and creating culturally appropriate open source theological education contents meeting accreditation standards. His only desire is that the churches in South Asia not only grow in numbers but also that their leaders and members become strong and healthy and deeply rooted in God's Word.

THE FAITH VISION

Dr. Raj testifies, "I earnestly hope and pray to see our nation transformed in my lifetime using the NPL movement. The Lord has also given me a vision and a burden to work relentless toward making at least the New Testament available in all the languages of our nation by 2025. The mission and the vision of both the Love Fellowship and myself is, 'A believer, a Bible, and a body of Christ in every language.'"

Notes

1. While Dr. Raj is a professing Charismatic/Pentecostal believer, not all who minister with him in Love Fellowship identify with that persuasion; his ministry is made up of both Pentecostal and evangelical Christians. The one thread is that they are all committed to Jesus Christ, are passionate about winning the lost people for Him, and planting new churches in unevangelized people groups.

2. Actual leader and ministry, but name is changed because of severe persecution of Christianity in the region.

3. Prayer walking is technically "praying on-site with insight." The believer walks through the neighborhood interceding for each house as he walks past its location. This is usually a daily routine.

SEVEN FAITH PRINCIPLES APPLIED

Chapter 11

FAITH'S CRUCIBLE

God uses the crushing experience of a long, cold midnight to motivate leaders to yield expressions of the lust of the flesh, the lust of the eyes, and pride of life, putting Christ first in everything and relying completely on faith to live for Him and serve Him.

WHY A CRUCIBLE?

"These trials will show that your faith is genuine....being tested as fire...purifies gold" (1 Peter 1:7 NLT). Men put gold ore into a crucible to separate pure gold from trash, impurities, and lesser grade metals. When the fire is stoked, first dirt is removed. The goldsmith sees trash float to the surface then is skimmed away. The fire is stoked higher as lesser grade metals float to the surface to distort the goldsmith's view. He keeps stoking the fire hotter and keeps searching to see something in the melting gold. Finally, when impurities are burned away, the goldsmith looks and sees his image in the pure gold. In the same way, our heavenly Father allows His servants to be purified in the crucible of earthly trials until He sees His image in your refined spirit.

Faith is purified in the crucible of pressurized human experience when the crisis of death, bankruptcy, prison, or extreme physical pain or sickness forces them to seek God and yield all to Him. The leaders in this book have all been through the crucible that has purified their faith and prepared them for service.

Suliasi, the Fiji government engineer who became a pastor and church planter, had his life changed by the death of a son. The excitement of nine months of pregnancy ultimately became a crucible of testing that motivated Suliasi to be a pastor and church planter.

David Sobrepeña was living the American dream as a stock broker with automobiles, a boat, a house, and retirement savings when God called him to return to the Philippines to plant a church. He gave it all up, sold everything, liquidated his bank and retirement assets. He entered a crucible of sacrifice that led to the largest born-again church in the Philippines.

Brian Houston was enjoying the prosperity of *second-generation faith* in planting a growing church when he was confronted with his father's sexual sin of abusing young boys in the father's previous church. The government accused Brian of failing to report the crime. The cloak of guilt was Houston's crucible, but God saw him through the testing to birth one of the largest faith ministries in the world.

On one of the first occasions when I met Jerry Falwell Sr., I wanted to write a story about his great church, so I asked, "Tell me how you got your great faith." Jerry had built one of the ten largest churches in America. I was writing the book *The Ten Largest Sunday Schools* (Baker Book House, 1969), and the pastors of the other nine churches had built on some other man's foundation. Jerry planted Thomas Road Baptist Church and built it from nothing to become one of the largest attendances in the nation. He had built this great church in a short period of time—16 years.

Jerry Falwell's answer shocked me: "I don't have great faith." He went on to explain that he only had average faith stating, "My faith is no greater than anyone else's faith." Falwell led me to believe he was not going to answer my question, so I put away my pen and closed my notebook.

Then he said, "Let me tell you about how I got faith from a great God." He explained that his faith in a great God didn't come easy, nor did it come primarily from all the great leaders he met at Baptist Bible College. The faith to build Thomas Road Baptist Church came hard and slowly.

One of the things we'll see in this book is that *crucible faith* came out through a time of testing, failure, severe pressure, when leaders were forced to rely on God more than any other time in their life.

Jerry told me that after he was saved in January 1952, he went off to Baptist Bible College to enroll as a freshman. His pastor, Paul Donaldson, had instructed him to get a Sunday school class, telling Jerry, "If you can build a Sunday school class, you can build a church."

So, Jerry Falwell asked Dr. Dowell, pastor of High Street Baptist Church, for a Sunday school class. The pastor sent him down to the basement directly underneath the church auditorium were Mr.

Max Hawkins, junior department superintendent, directed many small classes of junior boys and girls. When Jerry asked for a class, Hawkins looked at him skeptically, and later confessed to me his first impression of Jerry on the 30th anniversary class reunion of Jerry and his students. He said, "I didn't think he was able to build a class, and I didn't want him to mess up one of my good classes." So gruff old Hawkins said to young Jerry, "I'll put a circle of chairs over in the corner of the large assembly auditorium." Hawkins gave the college freshman a roll book with one name—an 11-year-old junior boy named Daryl.

The following Sunday, Jerry met Daryl and taught him the Word of God and challenged him: "Bring a friend next Sunday." Daryl didn't do it. I also talked with Daryl on the 30th reunion and he verified this story.

The second Sunday Jerry again taught the lesson, challenging Daryl, "Bring a friend." Again, he didn't do it.

At the end of the third week there was only one boy, Daryl. Jerry caught Mr. Hawkins going up the stairs to the auditorium for the church service and said, "You haven't gotten me any more for my class, so I think I'll look around for another ministry." Jerry held the roll book out to him.

Hawkins symbolically put both hands behind his back and scoffed, "I thought you wanted to build a Sunday school class to learn how to build a church." Then he quickly criticized Falwell, "If you can't build a class, you will never make it in ministry." At that, Hawkins reached out for the roll book.

"No, I'll build the class." Jerry quickly jerked it back. That was the beginning of Falwell's crucible of faith.

Baptist Bible College had classes five mornings a week, but no afternoon classes. Jerry got a key to an empty dorm room without a window; it was like a closet being used as a janitorial supply room. The room had an old army cot with springs without a mattress. Each afternoon Jerry would unlock the door, slip into that room, kneel down, stretch himself out on the springs, and begin praying for Daryl, many times for four hours. He agonized over his empty heart, begging God to help him build that class. He prayed for Daryl and all the other 11-year-old boys in the city of Springfield, Missouri.

The first day, Jerry prayed for 20 to 30 minutes, then decided to get help with his intercession. Jerry went to Mrs. Noel Smith, the librarian, and asked for some reading books to teach him how to pray to trust God for big things. On his knees, Falwell read about faith from some of the great works of Christian heroes— *Power Through Prayer*, by E.M. Bounds; *The Christian Secret of a Happy Life*, by Hannah Whitall Smith; *Your God Is Too Small*, by J.B. Phillips; *Spiritual Maturity*, by J. Oswald Sanders; *God's Way of Holiness*, by Horiatis Bonar; *Spiritual Secrets of Hudson Taylor*, by Dr. and Mrs. Howard Taylor; *Abide in Christ*, by Andrew Murray; *The Saving Life of Christ*, by Ian Thomas; *Bone of His Bone*, by F.J. Huegel; *The Pursuit of God*, by A.W. Tozer; *The Kneeling Christian*, by an unknown Christian; *Prayer: Asking and Receiving*, by John R. Rice; *Crowded to Christ*, by L.E. Maxwell; *The Pilgrim's Progress*, by John Bunyan.

In that room Jerry began following Jesus. As he denied himself, he yielded his self-will and ego-driven life. He picked up his cross—a prayer burden for ministry. But most importantly, Jerry sought and found the presence of God. "As I read the great stories of heroes of the past, I prayed for their faith and asked God to help me do the same thing."

On Saturday morning Jerry picked up Daryl in his car, "Let's go get your buddies." They went to every house where Daryl's friends were located, inviting them to Sunday school. Jerry talked to the mothers, telling them what time and where he was taking their sons to Sunday school. After Jerry exhausted the list of boys that Daryl knew, they went out to the fields and playgrounds to invite any and every kid they could find. "Are you a sixth grader? Would you come to Sunday school with me?' At 1:30 PM they went to the movie house where the local Saturday matinee was playing. They went down the line looking for anyone who was 11 years old to invite to the class.

Jerry had a new Buick Century car given to him by his mother. Also, his two roommates had cars. He would start out early Sunday morning like a giant train weaving its way through Springfield neighborhoods picking up boys for Sunday school. When the first car was filled, he sent it back to the church, then he would fill the second car, and then the third car. As attendance got larger, cars made multiple trips, and before the year was out the class had over 100 in attendance on several occasions, averaging 56 students for the year.

In the darkness of that college dorm room, Jerry found the presence of God, but more importantly he developed *crucible faith*, knowing God wanted to do big things with his life.

The whole purpose of *crucible faith* draws a leader closer to God, so He works through the leader to experience God's presence and power to accomplish God's work. In this crucible, the leader is separated from the world as he separates himself to God.

It is declaring that "my life belongs to God" and "my work belongs to God" and "my future belongs to God."

Faith's crucible is seen in the Old Testament where God sanctified (set apart) to Himself objects used for worship plus places, days, seasons, people, and leaders. So, today's leaders must apply the same priority as those in the Old Testament. They must put God first in their life to acknowledge God as the total Lord of their life and recognize Him as the source of blessing and expanded ministry.

Each leader will be "set apart" when they first come to Christ in their "initial commitment." But then they will experience "progressive commitment." This means progressive growth of the leader into the image of Jesus Christ. This progressive work can happen when a leader meets God in *crucible faith* and steps closer to God. Therefore, *crucible faith* is both initial and progressive.

The "fiery trial of faith" described in 1 Peter 4:12 primarily comes from the outside world or satan's attempt to attack you, hurt you, or get you to give up your faith. Peter fully describes, "That the trial of your faith, being much more precious than of gold that perisheth, though it be tried with fire, might be found unto praise and honour and glory at the appearing of Jesus Christ" (1 Peter 1:7 KJV). The description in this verse of "purifying gold in fire" is a picture of gold being refined in the fire of a crucible. *Crucible faith* is between the leader and God, not between the leader and his sin. It is not the world criticizing your sin, tempting you to give up and turn back. It is God pointing out your sin to draw you closer to Him.

Crucible faith mandates the leader draw closer to experience God's power. It is then God allows the Holy Spirit to reveal sin in his/her life, or God takes off the "blinders" and lets the leader see his/her sin. It is Isaiah in the presence of God crying out, "I am a sinful man. I have filthy lips...yet I have seen the King, the Lord of Heaven's Armies" (Isa. 6:5 NLT). Then Isaiah could properly respond to God, "Here I am. Send me" (Isa. 6:8 NLT). That is what God wants to do when He puts you in *faith's crucible*.

In the process of *crucible faith*, both God and the human leader are involved. As seen earlier, it is a human response to God that involves the three aspects of personality—knowing, feeling, and doing. The leader knows he/she needs more power and authority from God. Also, they know there are human issues, sometimes sins or disobedience, that are stopping God's blessing. Second, the convicted leader feels his/her failure or the ministry loses God's blessing. The emotion of loss of fellowship or failure drives them into God's presence to find Him and be empowered to serve Him. The leader's will is the third aspect of personality that motivates him/her to a decision. Here the leader decides to surrender all to Jesus Christ. (In one sense, no believer is ever able to yield everything to God because the human heart has hidden issues (see Jer. 17:9). Therefore, yielding is both the beginning action of giving all to God and an ongoing process of continually giving every new day, every new experience to God.

Notice how God used trials to prepare His servants to serve Him. Sometimes those who had the longest dark night rose to great usefulness for Him. Those who had the bitterest suffering were elevated to a height of influence. Those who apparently suffered the most were those who were used the most.

What is it about a long, cold, dark winter's night that prepares a servant to be used of God? First, some may be outwardly aware of some of their weaknesses, but in the darkness of despair they become acutely aware they have no strength to solve their problems. In the solitude of the dark midnight they wrestle with their faulty self-perception of who they are, of what they think they could do, and why they were put on this earth. After bitter internal defeat, they learn to turn only to God, to seek His will and strive only to give Him glory.

In a cold, dark night all doors of deliverance are usually shut. They learn they cannot help themselves; they cannot save themselves; they cannot do anything to change their destiny. Their only and final hope is God Himself.

On a dark, cold, winter's night they experience transforming power to give them hope, that God is the only One to transform their condition, and that His plan for their future is the ultimate purpose of living tomorrow. In that final hour, they yield to God, and as the deeper life leader once said, "They experience absolute surrender to God."

What was Jesus' condition for following Him? "If anyone desires to come after Me, let him deny himself, and take up his cross daily" (Luke 9:23). Jesus' invitation to discipleship involved the three steps previously mentioned. First, your act of the will to follow Him. Second, you deny the emotional impulses of self—self-exhortation, self-pleasure. Third, you are equipped to minister when you learn obedience from the suffering of your "cross" or hardship. The cross for some led to prison—or a martyr's death. But often, especially in our Western civilization, many seem to serve Christ without a "cross" or hardship. It may seem they have no outward suffering, but we don't know the depth or anguish in each person's discipleship, nor do we see their inner crucible that prepared them to minister for Christ.

A *crucible* is as a vessel used for melting or calcining a substance at an extremely high temperature. Actually, the word *crucible* comes from the same root as the word *crux*, which is something "essential to resolve a crisis." To some, their faith seems to grow slowly and easily, but to see the depth of suffering, consider the human heart is "most deceitful...and desperately wicked" (Jer. 17:9 NLT). Jesus said out of the human heart comes "evil thoughts, murder, adultery, all sexual immorality, theft, lying, and slander" (Matt. 15:19 NLT). Before being used of God, leaders must deal with any passions and deceptions found in their human heart. They usually do it in a long, cold winter's night—usually with internal suffering not seen by outsiders—before God can use them.

This suffering crucible is not the only thing to prepare a leader for service. But it is one factor, and unless a leader deals with their heart, their spiritual usefulness will be limited.

BIBLICAL EXAMPLE

There are some obvious biblical examples of crucible suffering that prepared God's servants for extraordinary ministry. Think about Joseph who was hated by his brothers, thrown in a pit, sold as a slave, and Pharaoh's wife lied about him, resulting in prison. Each and every suffering prepared him to be elevated by Pharaoh to manage the nation's farm harvest. He is credited with saving the world through a seven-year drought and famine. But most of all, he saved the Hebrew people.

Think of David being chased by angry king Saul for thirteen years. David lived in the wilderness and was forced to live in heathen cultures. All his hardships and sufferings were the seed that grew the man after God's own heart. His persecution was the seed bed for the greatest psalms to comfort those in affliction, preparing David to be the great godly king of Israel.

Think of God's call to Saul—who became the apostle Paul—who went into the desert (see Gal. 1:17), where some say he spent three years in isolation, and during these years of isolation he received revelations about the church as the body of Christ (see Eph. 3:1-5), and the riches of living "in Christ." After this Paul could only declare, "Not I, but Christ" (see Gal. 2:20).

EXAMPLES FROM CHURCH HISTORY

God has used *crucible faith* throughout the church ages to prepare His leaders for great ministries, perhaps greater than they could have had if they had not been stripped of egotistical pride, self-achievement, and any hidden rebellion to God's plan for their life. The way God used the people of faith in Hebrews 11 also applies to faith leaders in church history: "By faith these people overthrew kingdoms, ruled with justice, and received what God had promised them...their weakness was turned to strength" (Heb. 11:33-34 NLT).

John Calvin

John Calvin studied law before breaking from the Roman Catholic Church around 1530. Because of widespread violence against Protestant Christians in France, Calvin fled to Switzerland. There Calvin's faith was nurtured by this first crucible experience. He wrote his outstanding *Institute of the Christian Religion* and became a growing leader in the Reformation movement.

As a church leader in Geneva he regularly shared his ideas of a Christian city, but the governing council of Geneva resisted Calvin. He was expelled from the city, perhaps his second crucible experience, perhaps because he was rejected by the people to whom he was called and the people to whom he ministered. He went to Strasbourg, Germany, again becoming minister to the church for French refugees. This time he began publishing his commentaries on the Scriptures. Was this Calvin's dark, cold winter's night when he had to re-think his calling and readjust his approach to the church?

In 1541, he was invited back to lead the church in Geneva, Switzerland. He came back with new and more effective forms of church government and liturgy.

Ultimately Calvin developed worldwide influence on Reformed and Presbyterian type church movements, both in theology and ecclesial church government.

John Wesley

John Wesley ultimately became God's leader who established the Wesleyan church worldwide. Some have even suggested he was more influential on the Christian church than perhaps any other leader since the apostle Paul. At the beginning of the American Revolution there were 243 Methodist churches in the United States, but by the War of 1812 there were over 5,000 Methodist churches throughout the 13 colonies. What was the source of the spiritual power to build this movement? And how did God prepare Wesley to mold this movement into an aggressive worldwide evangelistic outreach?

The Church of England ordained only men who pastored churches. John planned to leave England, going to Georgia. John Wesley's mother, Susanna, went to the archbishop (leader of the church), pressuring him to ordain her son. But young John had no church. So, the archbishop ordained him "to the world." John Wesley went to the 13th colony, Georgia, with the blessing and ordination of the Archbishop of Canterbury. The well-known portrait of John shows his image surrounded by the motto, "ordained to the world." The archbishop was suggesting his ordination would apply to Georgia and not to England. But our Sovereign Lord would eventually use Wesley to send missionaries into all the world.

In Georgia, John Wesley, an unmarried man, followed the strict rules of the "Holy Club" learned at Oxford. While these rules embodied the best that legalism could offer, they didn't capture the power of the Holy Spirit, nor did they ignite a spiritual movement in Georgia. If anything, they led to John's failure.

In Savannah, Georgia, church attendance shrank under John Wesley's obsessive rules. At that time, he fell in love with young Sophia Hopkey, niece to Thomas Causton, official bailiff for the colony of Georgia. Eventually, young John proposed marriage and the couple became engaged. I am from Savannah, so I went to the Georgia Historical Society to read the actual minutes of the legal accusations brought against John Wesley. I was able to trace the actual places and events that took place.

After several visits to a river plantation owned by Thomas Causton, approximately five miles down the Savannah River, Wesley had an encounter with young Sophia in the plantation house that was never clearly explained. But a moment of passion gripped him, and whether he caressed her, or even touched her, is not known. Tormented by guilt, Wesley rushed out of the house, returning to the parsonage in Savannah. Young Wesley told the Moravian leaders about the encounter in their colony another five miles upriver. The leaders told the immature Wesley to break off all relations with young Sophia. They told Wesley the engagement was not God's will. He went back to Savannah and broke off the engagement.

Sophia was obviously embarrassed, so she fled to Charleston, South Carolina, and within three weeks she married. Then the couple returned to Savannah. Wesley sent a message to Sophia not to come to Holy Communion because her engagement and marriage had not followed the rules of the Church of England. She came to the communion anyway. Wesley refused to serve her the communion elements and publicly banished her from communion.

The uncle Causton was so enraged he formed a grand jury, made up of 14 dissenters (non-Church of England members), who heard witnesses, examined the facts, and brought 53 legal indictments against John Wesley. A few weeks before the trial, Wesley announced before the church that he was leaving the colony to return to England. He posted the time and date of his departure. The minutes of the town council said the entire population of the small town crowded around the river bluff on the appointed day, to see if John Wesley would be arrested or allowed to leave. John Wesley walked down the bank, hired the services of a boatman (a dissenter, a non-Church of England member), who rowed him on the South Carolina side of the river. It was a seven-day walk through the woods to Charleston. Wesley confessed on two occasions he got lost and would have died if God had not answered prayer and directed him to Charleston.

When Wesley boarded a ship for England, he wrote, "I went to Georgia to convert the heathen, but who was going to convert me?" (January 1738).

During the next two months John Wesley visited Herrnhut, Germany, a colony of Moravian believers who lived by the strict standards of holiness that John believed. After less than a week young John came away disappointed because he didn't find spiritual life in that "legalistic utopia."

A couple of months later on May 24, 1738, John visited a Moravian prayer meeting located on Aldersgate Road in London where he heard the readings of the introduction of Martin Luther's commentary on Romans. About that experience Wesley wrote:

> In the evening, I went unwillingly to a society meeting in Aldersgate Street, where one was reading (Martin) Luther's preface to the Epistle of Romans. About a quarter before nine, while he was describing the change which God works in the heart through faith in Christ, I felt my heart strangely warmed. I felt I did trust in Christ, Christ alone, for salvation, and an assurance was given me that He had taken away my sins, even mine, and saved me from the law of sin and death.

A short period later, Wesley encountered George Whitefield, an early friend from the Holy Club of Oxford. Whitefield told Wesley about the crowds turning to Jesus Christ among the miners (colliers) in Bristol, England. Whitefield told of preaching in the open fields. But Wesley rejected the idea, thinking that preaching must be in a sanctified church building, from a pulpit. He thought open-field preaching undignified and uncultured. Whitefield convinced Wesley that he could not know what God could do until he tried to feel the power of God.

Wesley stood on a small clump of ground outside Bristol, England, to meet the colliers coming out of the mines. Never had he met more un-churched, un-regenerate, unlikely prospects for salvation. They were tired, having worked all day, their clothes smelled with sweat, and their faces blackened with coal dust. But Wesley, with a renewed heart of the love of God—not legalism—preached to them with a new spiritual power he found in the Holy Spirit, and a new freedom he had found when released from the confines of restrictive legalism.

Based on his new *crucible faith*, refined in the fires of loneliness and failure, Wesley preached Jesus Christ. With the challenge of *brinkmanship faith*, he launched out to do what he had previously thought he couldn't do.

Wesley no longer could rest on his Oxford education, nor his handwritten sermons, nor his ecclesiastical garments, nor liturgical setting. A man who had been refined in the fires of Georgia perse-cution had come to the end of himself and was now captive to the Holy Spirit. He was released to preach the love of Jesus Christ to all, and that Christ had died for them.

Then Wesley records what he calls "Rivers of Revival."[1] The rivers were the tears streaming down the blackened faces of hard-ened laborers whose hearts had been touched with the love of God. The "Rivers of Revival" were not just about the tears on the faces of new converts; it was a river running in their hearts.

Now Wesley—a new man, with a new vision, a new methodol-ogy, and a new powerful motivation—wanted to reach the world for Jesus Christ. Now he would begin to complete the prediction over his life, "The world—my parish." Within a hundred years, the Methodist church he began became the largest in the world.

Billy Graham

Billy Graham has preached to more people in person and through media than perhaps any leader in church history. He has won more people to Christ than perhaps any other Christian leader. No one knows how many, because only God keeps those records. Perhaps all of this happened because a spiritual crucible took place in his life. Billy Graham's long, cold, dark winter's night of introspection, and futility, and searching changed his life and ministry. He met God in a new and unusual way. Two people who were at a dinner table that night that Billy Graham met the Lord told me this story, each from their perspective.

The two were J. Edwin Orr, a man with five earned doctorate degrees from some of the most prestigious universities in the world, also known for his research and writings on revivalism. He was Billy Graham's prayer partner in his first successful crusade in London, England, in the early 1950s. The other was Henrietta Mears, director of Christian education at the First Presbyterian Church in Hollywood, California, and director of Mount Hermon Bible Conference, and founder of Gospel Light/Regal Publishers, Glendale, California.

Charles (Chuck) Templeton was the third person at the table; Billy Graham was the fourth. Chuck Templeton was the conference speaker. Templeton was a Canadian who converted to Christianity and became an evangelist in 1941. He founded the successful Bay View Glen Church in Toronto and was associated with Billy Graham in the early days of Youth for Christ. Graham and Templeton went through Western Europe holding crusades in England, Scotland, Ireland, and Sweden.

But Templeton had taken theological studies at Princeton Seminary, becoming a theological liberal with serious doubts about the inspiration and authority of Scripture.

Templeton shared his doubts with young Billy at the dinner table, suggesting Graham's lack of success in evangelistic crusades was his attachment to old-fashioned fundamentalism with out-of-date illustrations and out-of-touch applications. Templeton suggested, "You must reach modern people where they are, speak about the power of positive thinking, give them a hope to improve their conditions, and build them up—and not tear them down with thoughts of sin."

At the table Henrietta Mears urged Graham to believe the Word of God. Mears went on to write the book *What the Bible Says*, which sold over 6 million copies, and was the teaching foundation of Gospel Light Publishing, becoming the third best-selling Sunday school literature among evangelicals.

Orr urged Graham to preach revival in our times based on "what God has done in the past...God will do it again." Orr urged Graham to preach, "If My people who are called by My name will humble themselves, and pray and seek My face, and turn from their wicked ways" (2 Chron. 7:14)—revival will come.

That night Billy Graham was thrust into *faith's crucible*. He went into the hills to search for God. Laying his Bible on a giant rock, he found God's presence. Struggling with the suggestions of Templeton to update his messages into modern terminology, Graham kept hearing Henrietta Mears talking about *What the Bible Says* and Orr's constant reminder, "Revival in our time."

Coming to the end of himself, Billy Graham surrendered to God on that rock. He suggested, "I will preach what the Bible says simply because God has said it, I believe it, and that settles it."

Graham concluded that if God can't bless His Word, there is nothing he could do to add to it. Graham determined his only message is Jesus Christ and Him crucified. Thereafter, Graham drove home the pronouncement in his sermons, "The Bible says."

He didn't always quote the Scripture reference, simply affirmed, "The Bible says, 'For God so loved the world that He gave His only begotten Son, that whoever believes in Him should not perish but have everlasting life.'"

WHY GOD SENDS A LONG, COLD WINTER'S NIGHT

Sometimes you arrive at a wrong doctrine or you develop a wrong understanding of doctrine or its wrong interpretation. God needs to teach you first to be loyal to Himself—to work for Him, not for your church or for your ministry. The cold, dark winter's midnight teaches you to get close to Him, worship Him, and enjoy His presence. Then you can serve Him properly.

Some are on the wrong path going in the wrong direction, and sometimes for the wrong reason. Remember Joseph suffered a long prison life in Egypt. Why? Because he bragged about his accelerated place above his brothers, and then his accelerated place above his father and mother. But Joseph was God's chosen man; God prepared his heart for greatness by teaching him obedience as a slave, and then he could rule an empire. Sometimes there may be disobedience in your life that needs to be corrected.

Sin is blinding, and when you are saved, God removes the blindness. But as Paul says, we only "see darkly" in this earth. Sometimes in human pursuits we allow compromise to slip in. You may not think it is sin, but what does God call it? If it is not in the will of God, whose will is it? So, God sends us into a cold, dark winter's midnight to root out any problems, any rebellion, any questionable behavior or questionable relationships.

Sometimes God sends you into difficult situations to teach you lessons you have not learned in your previous study or ministry. Maybe you need to learn what you didn't learn as a child or a teenager. Maybe it is what you did not learn as a young adult. God knows you and your future. He knows what you need to know and what you need to become to accomplish what He has for you. So, God sends you into a dark, cold mid-winter—not to hurt you, not to punish you, but to prepare you for a greater new place of ministry.

SUMMING UP FAITH'S CRUCIBLE

It's not enough to give everything to God; sometimes the Lord will test your decision to find out if you have honestly "turned from the past" and your "selfish ways." There are some who turn to Jesus Christ, but not with all their hearts, nor with all their souls, nor with all their strength. Your faith is tested in the crucible to see if you will depend upon God and Him alone for everything. The more you depend upon God the more you establish a relationship of faith and you are ready to work unreservedly with God and have Him work through you—whatever He wants to do.

Your dark night of testing will make you yield more of yourself to God than you have ever done. James says to let your test come, "For when your endurance is fully developed, you will be perfect and complete, needing nothing" (James 1:4 NLT).

God will use anything you give to Him, but the more you give Him, the more He can use. If you give God only 10 percent of your life, that is all He can use. But in testing you give God more than you have ever given to Him. So God uses *crucible faith* to accomplish more through you than ever before.

> "The world has yet to see what God can do with a person fully dedicated to Him." —D.L. Moody

Another thing about the cold, dark midnight of testing—God is teaching you how to do things His way, not your way. Notice how Paul described his testing: "But then something happened! God called me in His kindness...and undeserved mercy! Then God revealed His Son to me, so I could proclaim the gospel to the Gentiles. I did not rush out to consult with others about these things, nor did I go to Jerusalem...no, I went into the desert...it was not until three years later that I finally went to Jerusalem" (Gal. 1:15-18 ELT).

> Some faith lessons are learned only in your intimacy with God (revealing His Son to you). Some lessons are learned only from experience, not from books, lectures, or sermons. Some lessons must be tailored specifically to your new task and the new person you are to become.

Your night of testing will bring you to a place to make better decisions in keeping with God's person and God's will. But first you must make a one-time first decision to turn everything over to God. "Whoever desires to come after Me, let him deny himself, and take up his cross, and follow Me" (Mark 8:34). That first decision may come before your crucible-faith experience. Second, you will make daily, ongoing decisions to cause you to grow in Christ and ministry. These are the decisions that begin in your first meeting with Christ and may have been refined and sharpened by the experience of faith's crucible. These decisions represent a lifetime of walking with Christ.

When the crucible is placed in the fire, the heat melts the trash first, then the dirt, and next the melted iron floats to surface to be skimmed off and thrown away. Then silver comes to the surface, and the last is gold. The hotter the flames, the purer the gold. So, God allows us to experience *faith's crucible* to be used for Him in greater ways.

There is a second illustration of God chipping away the unused marble to find the masterpiece within the stone. Just as excess marble and dust was cast aside by Michelangelo as he was sculpting his masterpiece, the David, so will God chip away your excess baggage, habits, acquaintances, and sins to find in you His masterpiece—a faithful servant of God.

Note

1. Neil Anderson and Elmer Towns, *Rivers of Revival* (Shippensburg, PA: Destiny Image, 2019). This book describes the various expressions of revival. It is defined as "God pouring His presence on His people."

Chapter 12

BRINKMANSHIP FAITH

> In a time of crisis when ministry is stopped, a leader must turn aside from dangers or the issues that hinder the work of God and take a step of faith to solve a problem or remove a barrier by applying faith answers to the issue.

What is called *brinkmanship faith* in this book is called by others "a leap of faith." Many think it is the act of accepting or believing something outside the boundaries of reason. But remember, it is outside of the average human thinking or man's reasoning, but not outside of God's thinking. "My thoughts are not your thoughts, nor are your ways My ways" (Isa. 55:8). God goes on to say, "So are My ways higher than your ways, and My thoughts than your thoughts" (Isa. 55:9). So, when facing a *brinkmanship* issue, a leap of faith may seem illogical to the average person, but it may be blessed by God.

When Chris Hodges was frustrated with his ministry, in response to the call from God he launched out in a *brinkmanship* step of faith to plant a church in Birmingham, Alabama, where he knew no one. Today, the Church of the Highlands averages over 55,000 in attendance each Sunday.

When David Sobrepeña, a stock trader in Dallas, Texas, saw on television the People's Revolution in Manila, Philippines, against a corrupt president, he made a decision to sell everything he possessed, cashed in his retirement savings, and moved his family to begin a church back in his home country. Only seven people attended the first Sunday. But his *brinkmanship faith* resulted in the church today averaging over 60,000 in worship.

Suliasi Kurulo was a government engineer with a burden to win people to Christ. He purposed to knock on every door on his island in Fiji to present the gospel. Halfway through, he began a church, and together with the church he went to every home. When he buried his young son, he had a *brinkmanship faith* experience and determined to knock on every door on all the 300-plus islands of Fiji. Today, he has planted over 7,000 churches. Next, he plans to plant 100,000 churches in the islands and nation around the Pacific Rim.

But many leaders who have taken a leap of faith may not have seen the results they planned, or they didn't get what they expected. Sometimes they get the opposite of what they expected. Why? Because sometimes they get the natural consequences of broken laws. Or they lose momentum, or they lose the respect of followers, or they lose their entire ministry. When can a leader take a *brinkmanship* leap into the dark?

First, the credibility of the leap does not depend on the one leaping but on God Himself. Make sure God is speaking to you, and make sure you are applying all the other principles of faith.

Just because you feel a leap is proper and you have a burden to take a leap, that does not guarantee God is with you in your leap. Your leap must begin with God and must be motivated by God and must be based on God's principles. Ask yourself, "Is God speaking to me?" Many times you pray about serving the Lord, but it is possible to confuse what you want to do with what God wants done.

Brinkmanship faith begins when the Lord calls a leader to serve Him with a life-long commitment to full-time ministry, or it can simply be the Lord calling a layperson to a specific task or ministry. So, the first step is when a leader yields to the Lord and is filled with the Holy Spirit (see Eph. 5:18) and allows the Spirit to lead them in ministry or in a specific task in ministry.

The second step usually involves the Lord giving them a vision of what He wants to accomplish in that ministry or what should be done to begin the ministry (see the next chapter, "Reciprocity of Faith and Vision"). Sometimes ministry may be blocked with a problem or crisis. Sometimes there may be cultural or language barriers that must be crossed. At other times there could be financial or personal needs that must be solved. No matter the barrier that is holding back ministry, the leader will talk with the Lord and pray for guidance to solve the issue. Other times the leader will ask God to supernaturally intervene in the crisis or for Him to solve the problem.

The third step is when a leader must know and rely on the Scriptures and principles of faith to guide in ministry. Perhaps at this stage he must know and apply the biblical principles of dealing with crises or solving the current problem.

For the fourth step, a leader looks to his faith to guide his actions. Big faith must always be ready to go forward in ministry, but faith also must be willing to wait patiently for an answer before going forward. In either case, the leader needs to faithfully trust the Lord. There are times when it takes faith to patiently wait for God's timing; at other times, it takes *brinkmanship faith* to boldly step out in faith to go forward.

The last step of *brinkmanship faith* is when the leader makes a decision to act (an exercise of the will, based on information in the mind, and confidence in emotions); the leader then steps out in action.

Definition: Brinkmanship

Brinkmanship (Brink/edge–statesmanship), 1) the art or policy of pursuing or pushing a dangerous situation to the limit of safety, 2) the necessity of enduring danger to find a successful solution or place, 3) a dangerous solution or path when no other options are accessible, 4) a risky path.

BIBLICAL EXAMPLES

Perhaps one of the first *brinkmanship faith* examples was Noah, who followed God's call to action and acted on God's command. "It was by faith that Noah built a large boat to save his family from the flood. He obeyed God, who warned him about things that had never happened before. By his faith Noah condemned the rest of the world, and he received the righteousness that comes by faith" (Heb. 11:7 NLT).

The next example might be Abraham who was living in the city of Ur in the early civilization of the Euphrates culture. God called him to leave Ur and its surrounding advantages and go to a wilderness area to begin what we today call a *faith culture* (values, attitudes, and practices based on a biblical way of life). Abraham began the Hebrew nation. He not only had to give up his way of life and his extended family, but also give up his environment. "It was by faith that Abraham obeyed when God called him to leave home and go to another land that God would give him as his inheritance. He went without knowing where he was going" (Heb. 11:8 NLT).

There are some other examples of *brinkmanship faith* in Abraham's life. He successfully launched an attack on the kings of the Euphrates River Valley to rescue Lot, his nephew (see Gen. 14). Then Abraham had to send his son Ishmael and his mother Hagar away (see Gen. 21). His last *brinkmanship faith* act was when he was willing to sacrifice his son Isaac as a burnt offering (see Gen. 22).

There were many factors involved in Jacob's *brinkmanship faith* decision to leave his father-in-law in the Euphrates River Valley to return to his home in the Promised Land (see Gen. 29-32). One of those experiences was his all-night wrestling match with the Angel of the Lord (Christophany, an appearance of God), when he met God face to face. The next day, Jacob met with Esau, the brother he had cheated out of inheritance rights and property. Jacob thought his brother might kill him, because Esau had pledged to kill Jacob (see Gen. 24:11). Jacob went to meet his brother as an example of *brinkmanship faith* (see Gen. 33). But God changed Esau's heart, so they embraced.

Sometimes a *brinkmanship faith* experience will define a leader's *faith walk* with God and give direction for the rest of the leader's life or ministry. David was a 17-year-old shepherd, and only a few knew him as a musician (see 1 Sam. 16:21-23). David went out to fight the giant Goliath with his massive shield, armor, and sword. David had no armor, only a slingshot and five smooth stones. In this bold step into danger (*brinkmanship faith*), God used his few instruments (sling and stones), against the most fearsome enemy, the Philistines. David's practiced *say-it faith* when he announced, "You come to me with sword, spear, and javelin, but I come to you in the name of the Lord of Heaven's Armies—the God of the armies of Israel, whom you have defied. Today the Lord will conquer you, and I will kill you and cut off your head. And then I will give the dead bodies of your men to the birds and wild animals, and the whole world will know that there is a God in Israel!" (1 Sam. 17:45-46 NLT). The conclusion is well known—God rewarded David and he eventually defeated the entire Philistine army and became king of all Israel.

The New Testament brings us Paul the apostle who first stepped out in faith to carry out the Great Commission in Cyprus and Turkey (today's designation). He primarily went to Jewish synagogues, carrying the message to the "Jews first" (see Rom. 1:16). On Paul's second missionary trip, God gave him a night vision to leave Asia and go to Europe: "That night Paul had a vision: A man from Macedonia in northern Greece was standing there, pleading with him, 'Come over to Macedonia and help us!'" (Acts 16:9 NLT). Paul obeyed in *brinkmanship faith,* going to Philippi in Greece. "So we decided to leave for Macedonia at once, having concluded that God was calling us to preach the Good News there" (Acts 16:10 NLT).

There was no synagogue in Philippi, so Paul had to change his strategy and adapt his evangelistic methods to a Gentile culture that was different than the Jewish culture he previously encountered. Paul's *brinkmanship faith* resulted in the gospel leaving the Middle East, Asia, and going to the west, Europe. Sometimes the greater the challenge and the more fearsome the leap into the dark, the greater the results because God does a greater work in a bigger or better way.

TAKE AWAY

Brinkmanship faith is not an action you take apart from all other expressions of faith. It can be seen as the ultimate application of faith because all you are doing for God is cumulative, each leading to God's greater work in your life and God's broader work in ministry.

Chapter 13

RECIPROCITY OF FAITH AND VISION

> Faith involves seeing a need and determining a plan of how God wants that need to be met; as the plan becomes a reality, both faith and vision grow.

The "biggest" church ministry has perhaps the biggest ministry vision. Enoch Adeboye wants to plant a parish church of The Redeemed Christian Church of God within five minutes of everyone in the inhabited places of the world. They already have planted over 42,000 parishes, and in the United States 921 parishes as of Fall 2019.

Suliasi Kurulo wants to plant 100,000 churches in the nations of the Pacific Rim. The motivation that drove him to plant a church on every island of his nation—Fiji—is driving him to do it.

Dr. Raj wants to translate the Scriptures into every language in his nation that doesn't have a private copy of Scripture. He has planted 40,000 house churches and 5,000 street churches.

Both faith and vision are absolutely necessary to create a world-influencing ministry. There are three crucial steps for faith and vision to work together.

The first and absolutely necessary step to influence the world for God is vision that comes from God to change the world. This vision is as big as God Himself and as big as the world. When you know your vision is God-inspired, then you are ready to move to the second step, which is *faith application*. Both vision and faith are successful when they depend on each other and build up each other, i.e., *reciprocity of faith*. You must believe (faith) the vision is coming from God, and you must also believe (faith) God will use you to complete the vision. The last step is applying what is learned from vision and faith. Your application must work with God to influence the world or let God work through you to be a world-influencer.

Your vision and faith may or may not include when to start, how to accomplish the vision, what steps are needed to start, and what steps are needed to complete the goal. Also, this your vision and faith may not include who will help you, where the money is coming from to accomplish the vision, and many other small details. There will be many things you need to learn and apply to complete the vision. But when a vision is from God, it will grab you and make you a believer (faith), and these two forces (vision and faith) will motivate you to action.

This third step leads to eventual accomplishment. Your vision and faith will motivate you to raise money, recruit helpers, learn lessons, and force you to change your direction—even take detours—all with the purpose of accomplishing the goal.

If it is God's vision, it will burn like a fire in your soul, motivating you to sacrifice pleasures, past traditions, physical comfort, even financial security. You will not fear embarrassment, loss, and even death. If God has shown you a vision, you will assume Paul's attitude, "For me, to live is Christ, and to die is gain" (Phil. 1:22).

Definition: Reciprocity of Faith

Reciprocity: (French, re + pro) 1) inversely related, 2) constituting or resulting from one partner in a pair that supplies itself to the other, 3) serving to share or help both sides, 4) consisting of or functioning as a return in kind, and 5) mutually corresponding, i.e., mutual privilege to each other.

BIBLICAL REFERENCES TO VISION

Abraham's vision was among the first recorded in Scripture: "Sometime later, the Lord spoke to Abram in a vision and said to him, 'Do not be afraid, Abram, for I will protect you, and your reward will be great'" (Gen. 15:1 NLT). This vision told Abraham what God would do for him—protect him and give him a reward. In the same way, the leaders described in this book got God's vision of ministry—both what they should become and what they should do. Does God's vision to you include both? Remember, you will always do in ministry what you become as a minister for God.

When God's vision promised Abraham "your reward will be great," he immediately questioned God, "Since you have given me no children" (Gen. 15:2). Abraham reminded God of His previous promise: "I will make you into a great nation" (Gen. 12:2). Abraham knew a great nation should begin with a physical heir from him.

So, what did this vision from God and God's other conversation with Abraham do to him? Abraham's faith made him obedient: "It was by faith that Abraham obeyed when God called him to leave home and go to another land that God would give him as his inheritance. He went without knowing where he was going" (Heb. 11:8 NLT). The vision to Abraham produced his faith that carried him through various trials and failures.

When Moses met God at the burning bush (that was not consumed), God told him, "I have surely seen the oppression of My people who are in Egypt" (Exod. 3:7). Then God let Moses know what He wanted him to do: "I have come down to deliver them" (Exod. 3:8). Then God gave Moses a vision of what he was to do: "I will send you to Pharaoh that you may bring My people, the children of Israel, to bring My people out of Egypt" (Exod. 3:10). God was telling Moses to become the nation's deliverer. Moses was asked to do three things. First, deliver them from bondage in Egypt. Second, lead them through the desert. Third, lead them into the Promised Land. The books Exodus to Deuteronomy tell the story of Moses' task as he worked to complete this "vision" for his ministry.

When the prophet Isaiah was discouraged because his King Uzziah had died, God gave him a vision of what he was to do. First, Isaiah got a vision of the greatness and power of God. "It was in the year King Uzziah died that I saw the Lord. He was sitting on a lofty throne, and the train of his robe filled the Temple. Attending him were mighty seraphim, each having six wings. With two wings they covered their faces, with two they covered their feet, and with two they flew. They were calling out to each other, 'Holy, holy, holy is the Lord of Heaven's Armies! The whole earth is filled with his glory!'" (Isa. 6:1-3, NLT).

Second, after Isaiah saw God, he saw himself: "I am doomed, for I am a sinful man. I have filthy lips, and I live among a people with filthy lips" (Isa. 6:5, NLT). Your vision of God will always lead to a correct self-understanding.

Third, in the vision Isaiah was cleansed and prepared for ministry: "One of the seraphim flew to me with a burning coal he had taken form the altar...he touched my lips with it and said, '. . . your guilt is removed'" (Isa. 6:6-7 NLT).

The fourth and final aspect of the vision was a commission for Isaiah's service: "Then I heard the Lord asking, 'Whom should I send as a messenger to this people? Who will go for us?'" (Isa. 6:8 NLT). Isaiah answered God, as you must answer God when He gives you a vision of ministry, "Here I am. Send me" (Isa. 6:8 NLT).

God will give you a vision and you must respond in faith just as Isaiah. After you understand God and His nature, then you must understand your humanness and sin. Then you are able to respond in faith for cleansing and then in faith to build the ministry God has given you.

Chapter 14

OBJECTIFYING FAITH:
Say-It Faith

> When leaders speak or objectify what they want or what they want God to do, then God works the solution through the leaders and followers.

Jesus told His disciples that one expression of faith was to speak or say by faith what was needed so that it could be accomplished. Therefore, it is called *say-it faith* or *objectifying faith*. "Have faith in God, For verily I say unto you, That whosoever shall say unto this mountain, Be thou removed, and be thou cast into the sea; and shall not doubt in his heart, but shall believe that those things which he saith shall come to pass; he shall have whatsoever he saith" (Mark 11:22-23 KJV).

Notice five things in this passage. First, Jesus told them to have "faith in God." The Greek is *pisteu theu*—have God's faith. To move a mountain, you must have "God's faith," not your faith. Second, "Don't doubt." Third, focus your desire by faith on the things you want. Fourth, exercise faith that God will answer. Fifth, ask in prayer for God to move the mountain—solve the problem you face.

The leaders in this book discovered extraordinary potential when they said what they intended to do for God in their ministry. Their huge faith statements were more than wishful thinking, even greater than plans to get the ministry done. God had given them faith to believe they could do what God revealed to them. So they "said" what they intended to accomplish. Because God was in that *faith statement*, He helped them accomplished in action what they claimed in words. Their internal faith became *objectified faith*, giving them boldness to achieve what they conceived.

Leaders with great faith speak with great expectations. When Jerry Falwell was beginning Thomas Road Baptist Church in 1956, he made a faith statement, "I will knock on every door in Lynchburg, Virginia, to lead people to Christ." Then the church worship service was broadcast on television. "I will preach the gospel to everyone in Virginia by television." Then he made a *faith projection*: "I will preach the gospel to every home in America by television, and the program was broadcasted over 220 television outlets in America, covering 98 percent of the nation. Finally, in April 1972, he planned to broadcast the gospel by radio to every possible person listening to radio. The church spread the gospel by both television and radio, so time was purchased on every Christian international broadcasting station, and the church paid to have the sermons translated into every different language the radio used. While every person didn't listen to every radio broadcast, the worldwide attempt was Falwell's statement of *say-it faith*.

Enoch Adeboye, of The Redeemed Christian Church of God, Nigeria, has said he wants to plant a church within a five minute drive of every person in every major population center on the earth.

Suliasi Kurulo of Fiji has planted 7,000 churches in the islands of the Pacific and the surrounding nations of the Pacific Rim, but his *say-it faith* statement is to plant 100,000 churches.

Dr. Raj has planted 40,000 house churches and 5,000 street churches in his nation of South Asia, but his *say-it faith* statement is to translate the Scriptures into every language in his nation that doesn't have a New Testament by 2025.

Chris Hodges planted the Church of the Highlands, Birmingham, Alabama, and has an attendance of 55,000 in the main worship service and in 54 worship services. His faith goal—to plant a church in every populated area in Alabama.

James O. Davis began Global Church Network and has made a faith statement to motivate and synergize churches and ministries to preach the gospel to every unreached and unevangelized people group on earth with a view of winning souls to complete the Great Commission by 2030.

These are just some of the faith statements by leaders in this book. These faith goals are not motivated by bragging or self-advancement in the American entrepreneurial business spirit of building it bigger, better, and the best.

These leaders were called by Jesus to follow Him and carry out the ministry given them by their heavenly Father. They simply want to do what Jesus said, "Go into all the world, preach the gospel to all people, disciple them, baptize them, and teach them" (see Matt. 28:19-20). Therefore, out of complete obedience to Jesus, they have tried to do the best they could with the talent and resources given them. They have tried to do as much as they could, as fast as they could, as efficiently as they could. Their *say-it faith* passion grows out of their daily walk with and obedience to Jesus Christ.

Faith takes many forms, but perhaps one of the greatest expressions of faith is evidenced by a confident declaration of *say-it faith* that God will answer and that He will do it. How does this happen? Publicly tell what you expect to happen before it happens. Tell what will happen so it will happen. This is also called *objectifying faith*.

As Sunday school superintendent of the Thomas Road Sunday school, I met with the teachers and Falwell to set a goal for Harvest Day 1972. To my knowledge, no Sunday school had ever broken 10,000 in attendance. On a previous occasion I had said that 10,000 was a reachable goal, but I did not have faith to think that our Sunday school could do it. At the time attendance at Thomas Road Baptist Church averaged about 4,300.

That evening Jerry stood before a prayer meeting of students and church members to announce, "I feel God would have us accept the challenge of 10,000 in Sunday school."

As I sat on the platform, my first reaction was unbelief and fear of embarrassment. I was afraid of what people would think about my reputation if we did not reach a goal of 10,000 people. I had written books on Sunday school, but obviously I was not an authority on faith. I was beginning to learn the lessons of *objectifying faith*.

Faith is not just sitting back waiting for God to bring in people. The church organized the entire Sunday school for work. First, we asked 107 ladies each to take a page of a telephone book to phone everyone in the city and invite them to attend Sunday school. An invitation to the Sunday school was posted on twelve major billboards along highways into Lynchburg. Over 5,000 posters and handbills were distributed throughout the city; the teenagers also put them under the windshield wipers of every car in parking lots and on streets. Sixty radio announcements were made on every radio station, inviting visitors to attend Sunday school. Three letters were mailed to everyone in the Lynchburg area, inviting them to attend Sunday school. In addition to the other advertisements, over 200 people came out Saturday morning to visit everyone in the city to invite people to Sunday school the following day. On Harvest Day, *10,187* attended Sunday school. That great victory began with the principle of *objectifying faith* and was completed with dedicated human effort. Faith had conceived the goal, and faith had motivated the people to work. Faith had touched the heart of God to move the pastor and people to human effort.

AT FIRST, I DID NOT UNDERSTAND FAITH

Let's go back before Liberty University was started. In 1961, I became president of Winnipeg Bible College in Canada at 27 years of age. The school had an oppressive debt and there was no money to pay salaries. Everyone looked to me as the spiritual leader of the college to raise money to solve the debt. The school had a no-solicitation policy, technically termed, "full information without solicitation."

On at least two occasions I prayed all night that God would send in the money. Even though I was young at the time, age makes no difference in faith. My problem was that I did not understand the biblical principle of *say-it faith*.

First, I did not announce to the faculty, board members, or the student body that God was going to answer. In essence I did not "say unto the mountain, be thou removed." A second problem—I did not specify a certain amount of money. I just prayed in general for money. God honors all kinds of prayers, and some money did come in. But the victorious answer that I wanted was not realized. I grew a little in my faith, but I did not grow in a great way because I had not trusted God for a great answer to prayer. Later I learned *say-it faith* from Jerry Falwell (*transferable faith*).

We do not get *say-it faith* just by announcing a goal ahead of time. Many have announced a goal but have fallen short. Many have announced a financial need, but the money did not come in. There are biblical factors necessary to activate faith. First, realize faith comes from God, and only God can give inner confidence to trust Him for miracles.

Three Korean girls were attending a Christian camp somewhere in Korea. The stream that separated the camp from the small nearby town had flooded. The three girls needed to get to the town but could not cross the flooded creek. They knew the Bible story of Peter walking on water. The three girls knelt and asked God to help them walk on water. Then as a seal of their confidence, they told their friends they were going to walk on the water. They felt that they must demonstrate their faith because they had asked God for a miracle. When the floods subsided, all three bodies were found washed ashore downstream, showing God does not answer all requests even when one "says what they want" and "acts on their faith."

This story is a sad commentary of people who have misguided faith. But the worst results came when the newspapers printed the complete story on the front page, in essence mocking Christianity.

To the Koreans who are concerned about "saving face," the church was humiliated in the eyes of the unsaved. Therefore, it is imperative that when we exercise *say-it faith*, we make sure we follow all the principles of faith.

Many people express their faith as a confident feeling that God will do something. They convince themselves that what they want is the will of God; therefore, they say it publicly. But the answers do not come. *Objectifying faith* is a biblical principle but, like all truth, it must be harmonized with other principles found in Scripture.

Objectifying faith is also called "the word of faith" (Rom. 10:8). When Paul used the phrase "the word of faith," he is pointing to the spoken words of faith. There are two Greek terms for "word." The first, *logos*, means "a word as the expression of an inner thought." The other is *rhema,* which means "a written or expressed word, a part of speech."

When Paul said, "The word is nigh thee, even in thy mouth, and in thy heart: that is, the word of faith, which we preach" (Rom. 10:8 KJV), he used the term *rhema.* The faith of our heart is to be spoken by the mouth.

Later, when Paul said, "So then faith cometh by hearing, and hearing by the word of God" (Rom. 10:17 KJV), this term for "word" of God is also *rhema,* which means that people get saved by hearing or reading the spoken or written Word of God. The soul winners who are most effective are those who quote the written Word—the Bible—or they show the listener the Scripture in a Bible.

When a believer begins testifying to a lost person, they use *say-it faith* or *objectifying faith.* The written Word of God must be enlightened by the spoken Word of God. The Word of God gives eternal life, so those who base their ministry upon the Word—spoken and written—will communicate eternal salvation.

Objectifying faith involves the total commitment of the person to solve a problem. That person has confidence that God will do what He says. The old farmer was wrong when he said that "Faith is believing what ain't so." Faith is not just a leap into the dark. Faith is a leap into the light; when we step or leap by faith, we know where we are stepping because we are walking in the light of the Word of God.

Objectifying faith is not just human faith directed toward God. *Say-it faith* is a supernatural ability of God to plant faith in the human who trusts Him for marvelous results. The Bible teaches that faith grows from "weak faith" into "strong faith" (see Rom. 4:19-20). When Jerry Falwell first began his ministry, he could only trust God for $5,000 for supplies. That amount was needed so the men of the church could build an extension to the old bottling plant, a small concrete building approximately thirty by sixty feet, where the church was started. There was no space for Sunday school. So, evenings and Saturdays the laymen constructed the addition. Even as God was providing money for supplies, the children held class on a dirt floor. As Jerry Falwell learned to trust God for smaller things, God increased his faith. Before he died, he trusted God for a million dollars a day to keep the total ministry going. Now his son exercises *next generation faith* for billions of dollars.

The faith of Abraham was described as "not weak" (Rom. 4:19 KJV). He was approaching one hundred years of age and Sarah age ninety; the time of having children was past. Though Abraham had failed in his faith on other occasions, this time Abraham staggered not. The Bible says he was strong in faith (see Rom. 4:20). It is possible for a person to grow from "weak faith" to "strong faith."

Just as a church grows from victory to victory, so your faith may grow. No man becomes the heavyweight champion of the world unless he is victorious over every one of his opponents. He must go from victory to victory to become the world's champion.

To have *say-it faith*, we reflect the Lord God in whose image we are created. Concerning God, it is said he "calleth those things which be not as though they were" (Rom. 4:17 KJV). So, if we want to grow in faith, we must call those things which are not as though they will happen. Abraham had faith when circumstances were discouraging: "Who against hope believed in hope" (Rom. 4:18 KJV).

To have *objectifying faith*, we must have explicit confidence in the promises of God written in the Scriptures. Perhaps one of the best descriptions of *say-it faith* is, "And being fully persuaded that, what he had promised, he was able also to perform" (Rom. 4:21 KJV). Lest we think that the promises of God were only for Abraham, David, or other men of God in the Old Testament, Paul stated that faith is available "for us also" (Rom. 4:24 KJV).

TO TAKE AWAY

There are many ways to express *objectifying faith*. First, we can write a prayer list of what we want. The act of writing is an expression of our expectations. God, who knows all things, sees our penned prayer requests. But, more than the words, He honors the faith behind the requests (see John 14:14; Matt. 7:7-8). Hence, a prayer list can be an expression of *objectifying faith*.

A second way to express your faith orally is to a prayer partner or prayer team. As we tell someone our prayer request, we make a declaration of faith that we look to God and expect His help.

Then, in prayer, we articulate in words what we want God to do. The agreement together is *say-it faith*. Jesus said that, "If two of you shall agree on earth as touching any thing that they shall ask, it shall be done for them of my Father which is in heaven" (Matt. 18:19 KJV).

A third expression of *objectifying faith* is to give a testimony or to request prayer in church.

Another way of exercising *objectifying faith* is to set goals—attendance, financial, or others. Many times, church campaigns have an attendance goal, a financial goal for missions, or a goal to build additional space for the future.

Sometimes a missionary will share his financial need, in essence exercising *say-it faith* by trusting God and asking for support.

Another way of exercising *objectifying faith* is when you pray at the church altar. For many years those of the Wesleyan or Pentecostal tradition have invited people to come pray at the altar at the front of the sanctuary. Evangelicals have traditionally invited only lost people to come forward to be saved. In recent years, many have installed church altars to teach their people the altar is a place to get answers to prayer. Whereas many Christians may be reluctant to kneel at an altar during a church service, the public testimony of kneeling at an altar may demonstrate the credibility of your faith.

Say-it faith is not an instant solution to every problem, but answers come as a result of a dedicated life and knowledge of the Word of God. Actually, *say-it faith* is only one expression of faith, but perhaps the hardest to achieve in the Christian life.

Chapter 15

TRANSFERABLE FAITH

> The expression of faith found in great leaders can be communicated to aspiring leaders.

Did Chris Hodges learn it from Greg Surratt? Did James Davis use Bill Bright of Campus Crusade for Christ as his role model?

Enoch Adeboye's faith built the largest church in Africa. Josiah Olufemi Akindayoymi, founder and first Overseer of The Reformed Christian Church of God, is responsible for leading Enoch Adeboye to faith in Jesus Christ. The young man learned Christian doctrine as he translated the elder's sermons from his tribal language into English. *Transferable faith* was evident almost immediately, because young Enoch became active in expanding the ministry, adding more new parishes to the RCCG before becoming the next Overseer when the elder patriarch died.

James O. Davis began Global Church Network and acquired *transferable faith* from Bill Bright, leader of Campus Crusade for Christ, one of the largest evangelistic ministries in the world to college students. Did Bright give Davis the ability to attract over 200,000 churches and ministries from around the world, attempting to complete the Great Commission by A.D. 2030.

How does one get faith from another? Not every Christian leader with strong faith can communicate that faith to another person. Yet we see some examples where the strong faith of a leader is "caught" or "accessed" by a follower. Also, we see cases where "strong faith" produces positive results and is reproduced in a follower or one who wants to learn faith. On the other hand, we see followers learn extraordinary faith without a role model. They don't learn their exponential faith from another person, they learn it from God and the Scriptures (or perhaps they got exponential faith from a crucible).

When the Bible describes "from faith to faith" (Rom. 1:17), what does it mean? The Greek, *ek pisteos eis pistin,* is saying "out of faith into faith." The faith, *pisteos,* of the context is "salvation faith." Therefore, the text means out of your salvation faith you can grow various other expressions of faith, such as those being discussed in this book.

This means the phrase "from faith to faith" shows you can transfer salvation faith with your other expressions of New Testament faith. But, can this reference apply to transferring faith to others? Can those with faith to raise money reproduce *money-raising faith* in followers? Can those with faith to get victory over sin transfer *victory faith* to others? Another observation—does it mean those with faith to build a great ministry will communicate the same type of faith to another follower to build a similar type ministry, or in the case of *second-generation faith,* can the son learn the father's faith to continue building the institution by the same type of faith?

But quickly note, not all sons of great faith leaders have successfully led their father's ministry. Some sons have taken over their father's ministry, but the numbers went down, including momentum, money, and influence, etc.

One more observation, does the phrase "from faith to faith" mean faith can be transferred from one leader to another leader? Or could it be an extraordinary leader building a world-influencing ministry will transfer his faith to his followers, who together with the leader will build together the ministry?

So questions remain:

> Faith from leader to whom?

> What type of faith is transferred and what is not transferred?

> How is faith transferred?

> Why is faith transferred? What are the conditions in the leader and follower that make faith transferable?

> When is faith transferred? Is faith only transferred when a leader exercises his faith so that his expression of faith is transferred, or does it include transferring his total faith example to followers or other leaders?

> Motivation—must a leader desire to transfer his faith for it to be best transferred? If the leader does not intentionally commit to *faith transfer*, can his faith be transferred by observation and imitation, but without the leader's intention to communicate?

EXAMPLES OF SECULAR MOTIVES FOR TRANSFERABLE FAITH

Definition: Transferable Faith

Transfer: original, *trans-far*, 1) to carry or to bear, *move*, 2) to convey from one person to another, *transport*, 3) to cause to pass from one person or place to another, *transform*, 4) to take over the control or possession, *convey*, 5) to move to a different place, region, situation, *transfer*.

There are many secular reasons why someone will see faith in a leader and begin adapting that faith expression into their life. While these secular reasons will control the *transferable faith*, the next section will examine biblical teaching how faith is transferred.

Some secular reasons suggested:

> *Disconcerting or confusing ideas of faith*: This model says a follower can be confused or not understand faith or be ignorant about the biblical model of faith. But when they see successful faith in a leader, they will seek positive faith results, and *transferable faith* may occur.

> *Weak self-perception that leads to inability to believe/ trust*: Some have a weak ego (no self-assurance). As a result, they can't trust themselves, and this carries over so they don't trust God. But they can see the strength of faith in a successful leader and desire that

faith or desire the confidence or success seen in the faith leader. The example of strong faith in a successful leader motivates them to take steps toward learning and experiencing biblical faith.

> *Failure and guilt produce fear or inability to believe or trust*: Some potential leaders have experienced little or no results attempting to walk by faith or minister by faith because of inner fears or guilt from sin and/or personal failure. They are motivated by failure; hence, they can't believe or trust God. But when they see the success and confident faith of an established leader it becomes a model for their life that motivates them to a successful biblical faith experience.

> *The emptiness syndrome where some have never tried to follow God or never tried to step out in faith*: They will see the success of the faith of the established leader and a successful model will motivate them to acquire the same faith and follow the same principles that will lead to success.

> *Wikipedia suggests other ways social behavior is transferred*: These are the credibility of expectations, the power of leadership examples, persuasion by the leader, and sales presentation or marketing endeavors motivating followers to acquire the faith example of a leader to get the results the leader promises.

SPIRIT-MOTIVATED: TRANSFERABLE FAITH

When a successful leader exercises his faith in building a ministry and he brings his followers into partnership with him carrying out his ministry, the followers will exercise the same faith expression as their leader. As they exercise the same faith expression in ministry, their faith ability grows in them, producing *transferable faith*. Could this be one of the applications of Paul's expression in Romans 1:17, "from faith to faith"?

Just as spiritual gifts are given supernaturally by the Holy Spirit, so the gift of faith is given by God to His servants. At the same time, God uses others to be an example of faith, motivating them to acquire the same faith expression. It is God who gives us faith; God uses others to grow our faith, and God blesses their endeavor as we study to learn all we can about faith.

Transferable faith usually happens when a follower is influenced by the spiritual life and ministry of a leader who is respected. The testimony or example of the leader will motivate followers to acquire the same faith. This assumes the follower has a need to acquire faith from the leader.

Also, there is the *internalization of faith*. This is when the follower accepts and agrees internally and outwardly with the faith of the leader. This is much more than conforming to the expectations of the leader; this suggests the follower internalizes the ideas (biblical) and practices (Christian testimony) of the faith he sees in the established leader. Then he acts on faith, making it his own. When this happens, the leader's expectations of faith become the expectations of the follower.

BIBLICAL EXAMPLE

There are several examples in Scripture when faith was trans-ferable, but in some cases it was *second-generation faith*, such as Abraham to Isaac. But the relationship between the prophets Eli-jah and Elisha might be the best reflection of *transferable faith*. Look at how the two were connected. Elijah had been in ministry for years when God met him at Mount Sinai (*crucible faith*) and told him to wrap up his ministry by anointing several leaders to be kings in Judah, Israel, and Syria. But God also told the elderly Elijah to "anoint Elisha son of Shaphat from the town of Abel-me-holah to replace you as my prophet" (1 Kings 19:16 NLT).

These were two entirely different personalities, but the genuine faith in God was found in both. Elijah was a "loner" who lived in the wilderness most of the time. Even the name Elijah the Tishbite is suggested in the original Hebrew meaning "the stranger" or "the loner." In contrast, Elisha always had a group of followers with him; he lived in towns and he was often in the company of leaders, kings, or dignitaries. Yet the faith of both is evident in their rela-tionship to God.

Elijah performed seven miracles, while Elisha did fourteen mir-acles. While we do not compare the quantity or quality of their miracles, we recognize they both depended by faith on the same God for power.

There is no biblical record that the two traveled together or ministered together until the final day of Elijah's life. Somehow young Elisha knew God was going to take old Elijah to heaven at that time. "When the Lord was about to take Elijah up to heaven in a whirlwind, Elijah and Elisha were traveling from Gilgal. And Elijah said to Elisha, 'Stay here, for the Lord has told me to go to Bethel.'

But Elisha replied, 'As surely as the Lord lives and you yourself live, I will never leave you!' So they went down together to Bethel" (2 Kings 2:1-2 NLT).

The elderly Elijah tried to send young Elisha away, but each time the young Elisha said, "I will never leave you" (2 Kings 2:3-6). Then it seems the faith of old Elijah was transferred when he asked, "Tell me what I can do for you before I am taken away" (2 Kings 2:9 NLT).

The younger prophet wanted the evidence of faith. "Please let me inherit a double share of your spirit" (v. 9).

The elder replied, "If you see me when I am taken from you, then you will get your request" (v. 10). Both were talking about the supernatural power to be transferred to the young prophet.

Then the encounter took place. "As they were walking along and talking, suddenly a chariot of fire appeared, drawn by horses of fire. It drove between the two men, separating them, and Elijah was carried by a whirlwind into heaven" (2 Kings 2:11 NLT).

What can we conclude about *transferable faith* from this encounter? First, there was a desire of faith; both wanted God to transfer spiritual power from the older to the younger. Second, both made an expression of their faith—*objectifying faith* or *say-it faith*. Third, both had to act out their inner confidence. Elijah had to keep walking and Elisha had to keep following. This is almost an expression of *brinkmanship faith*.

One might go so far as to suggest a fourth expression—*living by faith principle*, which is described in the New Testament as *walking by faith*.

RESEARCH IN TRANSFERABLE FAITH

I wrote my doctoral dissertation on *An Analysis of the Gift of Faith in Church Growth*[1] for Fuller Theological Seminary, 1983, surveying 211 pastors in the Liberty Baptist Fellowship for Church Planting, 77 pastors returned their surveys. I asked each to assess their faith in church planting in four areas: 1) their faith that God called them to ministry, 2) faith for the location to plant a church, 3) faith in doctrine to be taught, and 4) faith in church objectives to guide their ministry. They were measured on a simple scale of one to ten, from weak faith to strong faith. What did I find?

Those with the strongest assessment of their faith built the largest and fastest growing churches.

Those with the weakest assessment of their faith had the lowest attendance and the slowest growth (or they closed their church).

As I interviewed ten of the graduates to write about their faith, I found their close reflection of faith expressions to Jerry Falwell, who planted and built Thomas Road Baptist Church. Many of the ten church planters told of being students in early chapels at Liberty University, where Falwell told about his experiences when planting and building Thomas Road Baptist Church. I found these faith expressions of Falwell duplicated in the lives of his students.

> Falwell's *crucible faith* experiences of being tried and tested were also evident in his students.

> Falwell's *brinkmanship faith* expression of launching out to build a church where situations and difficulties were many. Both Falwell and his students launched out in faith without a permanent location, with only a few

followers, with little financial backing, and against all odds.

> ➤ *Transferable faith* from Falwell to his students was evident. The ten Liberty church planters faced the same difficulties in the same way. They used the same faith expressions to guide their church from victory to victory.

> ➤ Both Falwell and the ten Liberty church planters used the same *tenacity faith* when defeated in a project, yet displayed continued faith to minister and build the church in spite of reversals. Falwell and the graduates continued to lead their churches to their next victory.

It is interesting to note that Falwell built his church using the same principles he learned from the leaders of the Baptist Bible Fellowship. He followed many of their same expressions of faith yet built a much larger and stronger church than any of them.

Beauchamp Vick, president of Baptist Bible College where Jerry graduated, was also pastor of Temple Baptist Church, Detroit, Michigan, with an attendance of 5,400 in 1969. There was a picture taken on the church's front steps in 1960 with over 5,000 in attendance, the biggest of the BBF churches. Yet Vick told me about Jerry in an interview in 1968; when he saw Jerry graduate he thought, "Jerry will either end up in prison, or build a church bigger than all the rest of the BBF churches." He said that because Falwell was always innovative and daring as a student. But Jerry was trusted to drive the pastors of great churches from the airport in St. Louis to Springfield, Missouri, to speak in chapel. Perhaps it was that four-hour trip from St. Louis where *transferable faith* happened. As Jerry talked to all the great leaders of some of the largest churches in America, perhaps it was there Jerry decided to build a large church—even larger.

Note

1. That dissertation was rewritten into a book, *Stepping Out on Faith*, in church growth language to contemporary pastors by Elmer Towns (Tyndale House Publishers, Inc. Wheaton, Illinois, 1984). Also see *An Analysis of the Gift of Faith in Church Growth*, a dissertation submitted to Fuller Theological Seminary, Pasadena, California, 1983, *Dissertation Abstracts*.

Chapter 16

SECOND-GENERATION FAITH

Second-generation faith is a commitment to the same values, attitudes, visions, and fighting the same battles of first-generation faith; but it adapts faith to changing culture and new emerging issues. Next-generation faith stands on the shoulders of the first generation to reach higher (vision), do more, and do it better in a new culture and for a new generation.

The following chart contrasts the differences between a leader planting a new church or ministry and the leader who assumes leadership of an existing church or ministry. The first-generation pioneering pastor usually begins with a vision of what the new ministry will look like on its first days and how it will look in succeeding times as the church grows. The second-generation leader assumes the ministry, and with it he takes on the vision of the pioneer who planted the church. However, the second-generation leader must analyze the strength of the organization and immediately begin managing its day to day ministry. The second generation will slowly define the vision, re-define the vision, and communicate the new vision to followers. All the while protecting the strength and stability of the original vision, while making changes to keep the ministry going in the same direction, fulfilling the original vision.

First Generation	Second Generation
Vision: finding new ministry	Analyzing and managing turf
Pioneer: originator	Settler: expand and plan
Innovator: change	Establisher: builder
Risk taker	Protect and multiple resources
Entrepreneur: self-reliant	Organizer: identify with project
Enterprising: make a name	Guarding the turf

The first-generation leader is the *risk taker* who usually is committed to the church and fulfilling God's vision. He is willing to launch out into the dark to get the ministry started. First generation leaders learn *crucible faith* through their difficulties and yield themselves completely to God and are willing to sacrifice everything for the ministry to go ahead. They love the challenge of walking on the edge between success and failure to get the job done. They realize if they hold anything back, they may lose their ministry, so they risk all to win everything. The *second-generation faith* is given the responsibility of people, ministry, property, and all assets. This leader will not risk all because it may not be his to risk. The second-generation leader is given the responsibility to guard the ministry, organize the ministry, and grow the ministry—make it bigger, better, stronger, and work to add other ministries to the existing ministry.

The first-generation leader usually has no one to help him or, if any, a few to help plant the church. The original leader must be self-reliant and be willing to do everything and have some ability to do all aspects of ministry. The second-generation leader steps into an organization already functioning. If he tries to take the tasks of others, the ministry may not function as well. The second-generation leader must recognize those ministering with him, work with them, and help improve them. The better he can manage/work through the existing work force, the stronger the church. The second-generation leader doesn't have to be as qualified in all ministries he oversees, but he must be better qualified at managing all, ministering through all, and getting all to work/minister together.

The first-generation leader will make a name/reputation because he has influence and he will be recognized as the founder of the ministry he planted. However, those with *second-generation faith* will not have the recognition enjoyed by the pioneer/founder. At the same time, he will recognize the founder and honor him for his influence on the ministry. *Second-generation faith* must build a reputation for the accomplishments of the ministry he leads. He must not focus on his own accomplishments, but he must focus on those in the ministry he leads. He must never get into comparing his reputation to the founder. The greatness of the founder is measured in the ministry he established. The greatness of the *second-generation faith* is measured by the strength he builds into the ministry and the accomplishments of the ministry.

BIBLICAL EXAMPLES

Abraham was the father of the Jewish nation. He exercised *brinkmanship faith* called "a leap into the dark" by leaving the civilized area of the Euphrates River Valley and going to live in the wilderness of Canaan. Abraham built an altar for the cleansing of sin and worship of God (see Gen. 12:8; 13:18). His son, Isaac, experienced second-generation faith by also building an altar to God for cleansing of sin and worship of God (see Gen. 26:23), just as Abraham had done. Also, Isaac's *second-generation faith* motivated him to experience worship in God's presence, as he re-dug the wells his father Abraham had dug (see Gen. 26:17-22). That also means *second-generation faith* today must depend on the same water of spiritual refreshing that refreshed and renewed the first generation.

Another biblical example of *second-generation faith* began with the successful *first-generation faith* of Moses (pioneering faith), with all his pressures, battles, and victories. Moses was seen lifting the rod to roll back the Red Sea. He was praying on the hillside with arms stretched to heaven while the battle over the Amalekites was being won (see Exod. 17:8-16). Moses smote the rock when the people were thirsty, and Moses was alone on Sinai, receiving the Ten Commandments. In the ministry of Moses, we see *crucible faith* and *brinkmanship faith*, when everything depended on him.

Joshua took over leadership from Moses. His *second-generation faith* is predictive of many of God's servants throughout church history who have had to take over the ministry of the "great" pioneering leaders, yet had a successful second-generation ministry.

There is another difference between their leadership styles. Several times there was rebellion to Moses' leadership. And Moses dealt with rebellion through the judgment of God. But at the same time there was no record of rebellion to Joshua's leadership. General Joshua is seen behind the scenes, directing battle strategy to accomplish victory through his followers.

The leadership skills of the first generation required personal strength and complete confidence in God. The second-generation leader must know his organization (strengths and weaknesses), know the ministry goals, and use vision and management skills to guide the entire work force to complete the goals of ministry.

The same comparison can be made between the apostle Paul, who was the pioneer planting the "Gentile" church throughout the Roman Empire, and Timothy who ministered with Paul, then had to carry on Paul's tradition after martyrdom.

Paul was the first-generation leader who demonstrated entrepreneurial leadership skills and had all the characteristics of *first-generation faith*. He learned faith originally in the crucible of the desert (see Gal. 1:17). Paul also developed his faith in the prison of Philippi and several other times he was persecuted and tortured (see 2 Cor. 4:8-19; 6:3-10). Also, Paul exercised *brinkmanship faith*.

But Timothy had *second-generation faith*. He was converted on Paul's first trip to Lystra, and joined him on his second journey (see Acts 16:1-5). Paul went to prison, was beaten and suffered, but Timothy didn't go to prison. Also, Timothy was there watching when Paul was stoned to death (see Acts 14:19-20). But second-generation Timothy served as pastor of the church established by Paul (see

TEN *of the* LARGEST CHURCH MINISTRIES AGGRESSIVELY TOUCHING THE WORLD

2 Tim. 1:5-7). Whereas Paul carved the church out of raw heathen ingredients, Timothy shepherded the flock, protected the flock, and fed the flock. Paul and Timothy had the same faith, but they had to express it differently. Didn't Paul say, "I planted the seed" (1 Cor. 3:6 NLT)? He went on to explain that it's not important who does the watering—God makes the seed grow (see 1 Cor. 3:7).

EXAMPLES FROM HISTORY

Church history continues to remind us of bold pioneering leaders who blazed new trails for God, carving out new ministries from heathen cultures, building Christian ministries for God. Bold Martin Luther in Germany brought the Lutheran church out of Roman Catholicism and was followed by Philip Melanchthon, the second-generation educator.

John Wesley laid the foundation for the Wesleyan church in England that became the greatest church movement to emerge on the scene since the apostle Paul. After Wesley's death, Francis Asbury symbolically "rode" his horse to establish the Methodist church to unparalleled advances in America, evangelizing every one of the 13 colonies.

For the example of many successful second-generation leaders, there also is a trail of those who followed great leaders but couldn't keep growth momentum. These second-generation leaders either plateaued or allowed ministries, churches, and finances to decline.

The classic Scripture to describe the plight of second-generation leaders and followers is: "After that generation died, another generation grew up who did not acknowledge the Lord or remember the mighty things he had done for Israel. The Israelites did evil in the Lord's sight and served the images of Baal. They abandoned the Lord, the God of their ancestors, who had brought them out of Egypt. They went after other gods, worshiping the gods of the people around them. And they angered the Lord" (Judg. 2:10-12 NLT).

Second-generation faith does not mean it is worn out faith, as we might buy old clothes from a second-hand shop to get some more life out of them after the original owner used the garments. No, not at all. *Second-generation faith* can be stronger than the original faith of the first generation and can do more or do it better.

But in Joshua, there is a different style of leadership and a different expression of faith. Moses and Joshua had the same faith, the same focus on God, and the same relationship to God. But when Joshua faced Jericho, he had the priests march around the city. Joshua was the leader, but didn't stand out individually as Moses, "Joshua commanded the people, 'Shout!'" (Josh. 6:16 NLT). But also when Israel sinned (see Josh. 7:1-26), it was a team response. "Joshua and the elders of Israel tore their clothing" (Josh. 7:6 NLT). *Second-generation faith* focuses on the effectiveness of corporate leadership.

Second-generation Timothy had to lead a church through second-generation issues. His *second-generation faith* was God's way of growing the second-generation Christians in Ephesus.

SOCIOLOGICAL CYCLE OF GENERATIONAL CHURCHES

This chapter suggests Christian ministries and churches reflect the theological and sociological posture of the church's position on the sociological cycle. 1) Newly planted churches and ministries have the capacity for the fastest growth, although not all fundamentalist churches are growing. The ten churches and ministries of this book are found at the first stage of the cycle. 2) Second-generation churches have capacity for growth, although not as fast. Also, not all second-generation churches/ministries are growing. They usually do not have the spiritual dynamic to attract individuals. When the attendance at second-generation churches/ministries grows, it does so by the outreach of members, not necessarily driven by the second-generation leader. Most denominational-type churches/ministries do not grow because they apply no external pressure for growth or their spiritual life is weak; hence, they have no internal dynamic for growth.

Sociological Cycle

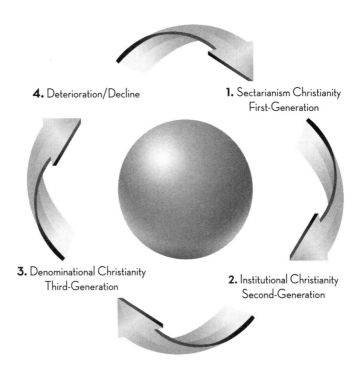

4. Deterioration/Decline

1. Sectarianism Christianity
First-Generation

3. Denominational Christianity
Third-Generation

2. Institutional Christianity
Second-Generation

David Moberg, the church sociologist from Marquette University, has designed the cycle "as a process by which cults originate, develop into sects, and then change into denominations, perhaps finally to emerge from the process as churches."[1]

Ernst Troeltsch, the German philosopher-sociologist, wrote almost 150 years ago that churches grow from a sect status to *ecclesia* (church stage) to a denominational stage.[2] The above cycle is an elaboration of Troeltsch's position to show the church's sociological cycle. A church begins as a sect and moves to become church at the second stage on the cycle—a second-generation institution. The third stage on the cycle is a fully organized denomination, and the final stage is deterioration.

In this chapter the sect will be associated with first-generation ministry. The second stage of the cycle called the institution will be identified with second-generation Christian ministries. *Denominationalism* will be associated with the ministries that have lost their vision and purpose.

A COMPARISON OF FIRST-GENERATION FAITH WITH SECOND-GENERATION FAITH

Both leaders—first- and second-generation leaders—must have the same faith for God, because faith is the relationship to God, and both leaders must come to God, trust God, lean on God, and accept God's strategy of faith and apply faith to their life. Yes, both first and second-generation have faith, and their faith when examined under the microscope is the same—the same essence.

But they usually express their faith differently because the first generation is building a church in a non-Christian culture. The new church culture is different from the previous life of new converts. The second generation is building up the structure of the church/ministry established by the leader or the first-generation founder. As a matter of fact, there are different applications of faith between first and second generation. You can examine them, but always understand they both have the same faith and same God, and their faith in God is the same but their expression of faith may be different.

When times change, needs and culture changes. There is a great difference between a young sapling tree, one or two years old, compared to a mature tree growth 40 years later—the same tree, same consistency of wood, limbs, leaves, sap, etc., but what is different? How the tree reacts to wind, the amount of fruit it produces, the ability to survive extreme weather and disease, and how the tree interacts with the environment (culture). Probably the forest where the old tree is growing is different from the forest 40 years ago. It is the same way for the first- and second-generation ministry leader. Leadership is applied in many different ways. Note the following.

1. The first-generation leader focuses on individuals while the second generation focuses on the organization of teams, committees, and boards to establish policies and minister to individuals.

Many times, the first-generation pastor knows everyone in the church by name, and on some occasions he has seen them walk the aisle to be converted or he may have actually led them to Christ in their homes. He has visited them when they are sick and counseled them when they had a problem, and he rejoices with them on achievements or victory. As the church/ministry becomes larger, the second-generation leader with faith may not know everyone in the church although he will know certain individuals because of their position or for other reasons. Many times the number of people may prohibit the second-generation leader from knowing or becoming intimately involved and relating to everyone in a large church/ministry.

The second-generation leader will use organizational faith to put the right person in the right ministry (committee), doing the right task that fulfills their goal and spiritual giftedness. The second-generation leader will try to get everyone working together in harmony and efficiently. Many times, the first-generation leader moves the church by his work or the work of individuals, while the second-generation leader works through committees and boards to keep everyone focused for the church/ministry purpose.

2. The effectiveness of first-generation leadership is usually measured by growth, problem solving, new programs, new facilities, and addition of new workers. The second generation is measured by stability, influence, and effectiveness of each section of the organization that contributes to the effectiveness of the whole church/ministry.

The leader of a growing church/ministry will focus on those individuals who are producing ministry and carrying out institutional purposes, at the same time recruiting, training, and motivating leaders to further the church/ministry. The second-generation leader must keep his eyes on the larger picture of the total church/ministry as it works toward its goals, working with the committee/board so that each contributes a fair share of growth and enrichment with harmony and unity.

The first-generation leader will perhaps produce the fastest and most growth of ministry/church while the second-generation leader must give attention to unity, stability and effectiveness so everyone is working together, all committees are making their ministry contributions, and the church is moving forward to its intended goal.

3. First-generation leaders strive against outward sin(s) that reflects culture, because the world is not a friend of God or any aggressive advances of His work. The first generation may be opposed by media, business, or even civil institutions. The second-generation leader will usually assume leadership of an influential church/ministry that has carved its existence into the culture of community and has established co-existence with other institutions in the community. As the first-generation leader strives to give his church/ministry life and effective outreach, he will grapple with both social and civil laws that would hinder growth. He must use Christian principles in dealing with opposition, at the same time always leading his people to growing a successful ministry that is seen as victorious over opposition.

The second-generation leader must work with and through existing culture, represented by systems, while ministering through political, financial, and social communities.

4. The first-generation leader usually measures the loyalty of his followers by their enthusiasm; involvement; attendance; giving of time, talent, and treasure; and support to the institution and to the leaders. However, the second-generation leader primarily measures the loyalty of followers by their loyalty to the institution and their involvement in group ministry that contributes to its health, progress, and stability.

5. The first-generation leaders may measure their efficiency by their relationship to Christ and by their personal involvement of giving of time, talent, and treasure to Christ. The second-generation leaders probably measure their effectiveness by loyalty to both Christ and the church/ministry. Also, obviously, giving time, talent, and treasure.

6. The first-generation leaders prize measured growth of the church/ministry toward its goal. The second-generation leaders prize the effectiveness of the church/ministry as seen in efficiency and development of members in the life and outreach of the church.

7. First-generation leaders tend to be more emotional in their appeal to the followers, while second-generation leaders appear to be more rational in motivating followers in their relationship to ministry, worship, and fellowship.

8. First-generation leaders are more ready and more likely to fight or attack existing evil systems (politics, religion, economics, etc.), knowing if they don't win this battle the life of the church will be threatened. However, the second-generation leaders usually do not fight existing institutions, because these battles have been won, but will work with institutions sometimes in small committees or behind closed doors to further the cause of the ministry.

Notes

1. David O. Moberg, *The Church or a Social Institution* (Englewood Cliffs, N.J.: Prentice-Hall, Inc., 1962), 100.

2. Ernst Troeltsch, *The Social Teaching of the Christian Churches*, trans. by Olive Wyan (London: George Allen and Unwin, 1931), 2 vols. An outstanding analysis of the factors that cause deterioration in churches.

Chapter 17

THE GIFT OF FAITH

> True faith is the most active motivating power in the whole world. "Faith, which worketh by love," works all sorts of marvels; and where there is this true faith, it will prove its reality by its practicalness.
> —Charles Spurgeon

The leaders in this book seem to have greater faith then the average Christian; at least, their faith has greater results. They are planting and building some of the greatest ministries in history. Do they have a special gift—a gift of faith?

We must understand the nature of the spiritual gift of faith if we want to move mountains. Paul wrote, "And though I have the gift of prophecy, and understand all mysteries and all knowledge, and though I have all faith, so that I could remove mountains, but have not love, I am nothing" (1 Cor. 13:2). Paul was referring to Jesus' statement, "Have faith in God...you can pray for anything, and if you believe that you've received it, it will be yours" (Mark 11:22,24).

Some people obviously have more faith than others. As we study the Bible, we see some men accomplish great tasks by faith. Abraham was one hundred years old, yet miraculously fathered a child. Through faith he overcame the barrenness of Sarah's womb. Could we trust God for a similar miracle? Probably not!

Moses stood before the multitude and commanded, "Stand still and you shall see it come to pass." By faith he knew that God would roll back the waters of the Red Sea; therefore, he exercised the spoken word of faith. We probably could not do that either!

Some might say that it was easy for people in biblical times to have faith. They heard the actual voice of God or they saw his angel. They experienced the miracles of God. Why should they not have faith? Yet, we seem to have no supernatural basis for faith.

But does God still speak to us through the Scriptures? Remember the Bible is the greatest miracle that God has given to us. God performed a miracle by inspiring and preserving the Bible. Is the supernatural Bible our basis for claiming the work of God by faith?

How can one man, Enoch Adeboye, make such a big difference so that over 42,000 churches are planted by his church ministry? Is it his faith? Is it his organizational or management ability? Is it primarily the power of the gospel and not the power of Adeboye's faith? Or a combination of all these factors?

Look at the enormous success of Hillsong. Is it the power of Houston's faith? Did he touch a "worship" nerve in evangelical Christianity? Was it just God that expanded the work by television?

As you analyze the accomplishments of the ten church ministry leaders, what role did their faith have in the success of their results? Did God sovereignly give them their spiritual gift of faith?

Or did they acquire more faith by their obedience to biblical truth, thus leading to more usefulness by God?

The Bible describes the extraordinary gifts given to some people to serve God. These spiritual gifts are a person's ability to accomplish the work of God. In our day, these are usually called "serving gifts." Some of them are described as preaching, teaching, serving, or the gift of administration (see 1 Cor. 12:8-11; 28-30; Eph. 4:11; Rom. 12:6-8). However, the Bible seems to identify faith as one of the "serving gifts" given by the Holy Spirit to believers. Paul says, "To another faith by the same Spirit" (1 Cor. 12:9). Because faith appears in the list of spiritual gifts, it is apparently not a reference to saving faith.

In another place, Paul listed the gift of faith with the gift of preaching (prophecy): "Having then gifts differing according to the grace that is given to us, let us use them: if prophecy, let us prophesy in proportion to our faith" (Rom. 12:6). Some are not sure whether the word "faith" in this verse is used to describe the preacher's faith to use his preaching, or whether Paul is saying that faith is a special gift given independently of preaching. If faith is separate from preaching, it means that a person could serve God by using faith to plant a church ministry or using faith to get results in a soul-winning campaign.

Again, Paul compares the gift of faith to love: "And though I have the gift of prophecy, and understand all mysteries and all knowledge, and though I have all faith, so that I could remove mountains, but have not love, I am nothing" (1 Cor. 13:2). The gift of faith is listed with the gift of prophecy, giving the ability of faith equal status with the ability to prophesy, i.e., to preach. The one who "moves the mountain of unbelief" is just as important as the one who preaches the Word of God.

When Paul said "all faith" (1 Cor. 13:2), he probably included more than a reference to the seven different expressions of faith mentioned in the Appendix. "All" probably includes the object of faith (faith and its object cannot be separated), so Paul was saying that if all barriers were removed by faith and all things could be accomplished by faith, the results are nothing without love.

Because First Corinthians 12 was written to explain to Christians their spiritual gifts, we can only conclude that faith is a special ability given to some people to serve God. These ten leaders seemed to have more faith than anyone else. Is the basis of this statement their supernatural gift of faith? But you should not give up because of your lack of faith. The Bible teaches that anyone can grow whatever gift they have by following God's rules concerning the spiritual gifts.

To understand the nature of spiritual gifts, we must understand that there were different kinds of gifts and different levels of effectiveness given to different people (see 1 Cor. 12:4-6). Paul explained this by stating: "Having then gifts differing according to the grace that is given to us" (Rom. 12:6).

Jesus was teaching us about gifts when He gave the parable of the talents. It is more than a coincidence that one man was given five talents, the second two talents, and the last man one talent. It is very obvious that the Lord gave a different gift to each man, illustrating the fact that the Lord gives different spiritual gifts to people. It is also not a coincidence that the word *talent* (a weight of precious metal, silver or gold) in the parable actually came to mean in English "abilities." A gifted person is also talented.

Actually, a talent, in a parable, was $10,000 if it was silver. If it was a talent of gold it would have been worth over $750,000.

The person with one talent might be similar to a new Christian who has only one talent of serving Jesus Christ by cutting grass, sweeping out the classroom buildings, or washing windows in the church. The five-talent Christian is similar to those who preach in churches, have a knowledge of Scripture, and are wise in ministering to people. Everyone has a different number of talents, and the effectiveness of each spiritual gift is different. Therefore, some might have a greater gift of faith, while the next person does not. And some will have more faith to do more for God than others.

The spiritual gifts are also qualitative in usefulness, meaning two leaders might have the same gift, but one has a greater use of that gift than the second. As an illustration, some who have the gift of teaching are more effective than others who teach the Word of God. The spiritual gift of teaching is not measured by how many pass or fail a course, but how deeply the lives of students have been changed. Some with a greater gift of faith lead their ministry to greater results than others. Paul evaluated the effectiveness of a spiritual gift as "the manifestation of the Spirit" (1 Cor. 12:7). When a spiritual gift is properly exercised, the Holy Spirit will manifest Himself in the lives of the hearers through the fruits of the Spirit, such as love, joy, and peace (see Gal. 5:22-23). Can we assume when the church grows and more people are manifesting the Holy Spirit by love, joy, and peace, it was because the leader had more faith to trust God for a bigger harvest of souls?

Therefore, we understand why some have more results in serving God than others—it is because they have more spiritual gifts or a manifestation of their spiritual gift. Will an effective soul winner be able to win more to Christ than those with less faith? Does he have the gift of faith to trust God for lost souls to get saved? Or was it a greater spiritual gift of evangelism? Was it because his faith got him up each morning at five o'clock praying for lost peo- ple? Or was it because he diligently presented the gospel to lost people. Was it a mix of the gift of evangelism with the gift of faith and, as a result, many were won to Jesus Christ?

So where does that leave you? As some outstanding leaders have more spiritual gifts, or a greater gift of faith, should you give up? No! But some give up because they think they do not have the gift of faith. They think they cannot trust God to "move moun- tains." A careful study of spiritual gifts will reveal that God is not partial. What He has done for one leader, He can do for you...if you are willing to learn the same lessons.

Paul taught that we should "Covet earnestly the best gifts" (1 Cor. 12:31 KJV). This means that you can desire the best gifts that God has to offer. If you feel that preaching is the best gift, you should pray and ask God to increase your ability to preach. In another place Paul exhorted, "If a man desire the office of a bishop, he desireth a good work" (1 Tim. 3:1 KJV). Therefore, it is only natural that a great leader of God would have great dreams/ visions serving the Lord through a greater exercise of his leader- ship ability. If you desire faith like Paul or Moses, rejoice, for faith can come with desire.

But some will say that the gifts are only given sovereignly, that God controls both the choice and the gift itself. But Dr. Charles Ryrie, former professor of theology at Dallas Theological Seminary, responded, "If God gives you a spiritual gift, He will also give you a desire to use it." Therefore, if you have a desire for more faith, it is evident that you probably have a greater gift of faith in your heart.

Because we are children of God, we are saved by faith, and with that salvation we have the faith of God in our hearts. The

Bible teaches that Jesus Christ provided for the spiritual gifts at salvation: "When he ascended up on high, he led captivity captive, and gave gifts unto men" (Eph. 4:8 KJV). This reference to the resurrection appears in the center of the passage on spiritual gifts, teaching that spiritual gifts were bestowed embryonically at the resurrection of Christ. All are not equal in gifts, but we can grow in our gifts that Jesus gave us. You have the gift of faith in latent form in your heart, so now God expects you to exercise your faith so it will grow.

In the parable of the talents, the man who was given five talents used them wisely. When the lord returned, he was given five other talents, making a total of ten talents. Faithfulness in the use of small gifts leads to a larger sphere of service. The man who faithfully teaches a Sunday school class of small children may be preparing himself to preach in the jails or at a rescue mission service. He who leads a church faithfully is preparing for greater leadership and a greater ministry.

We should examine our spiritual gifts. Perhaps we have the gift of faith and are not exercising it properly. Paul exhorted, "Now concerning spiritual gifts, brethren, I would not have you ignorant" (1 Cor. 12:1 KJV). We should not be ignorant of our gifts, nor of what we can do for God. The proper use of our spiritual gifts will lead to greater usefulness, so we can have a more profitable life for God by faithfully doing the small thing today. And as Christians grow on victories, so we will grow "from faith to faith" (Rom. 1:17).

Section Three

APPENDICES

Appendix A

WHY FAITH GROWS CHURCHES AND MINISTRIES

New churches and ministries are born of God by leaders of faith, usually unheralded by the world. These are God-called leaders, anointed to build one church or a ministry of churches. Their churches and ministries are the extension of visions and outreach of their faith that planted them to carry out the Great Commission around the world.

What kind of a man determines to knock on every door on his island in Fiji to tell everyone about Jesus Christ? Halfway through the island, this man of faith planted a church that helped him reach everyone on his island. Then his faith drove him to move to the capital of Fiji to begin a church. His faith continued to drive him to knock on every one of the 300-plus Fiji Islands. So, he planted churches on every island and through these new churches, someone knocked on every door on every island.

His faith motivated him to initiate a Bible school to train church planters to plant churches outside the island of Fiji. His faith motivated him to begin an international organization that has planted over 7,000 churches around the Pacific Rim. If you could understand the type of faith that motivated Suliasi Kurulo you would understand his vision to plant 100,000 churches throughout the world. If you understood that then, you know *extraordinary faith* is available to you.

A man of faith who begins a church to reach his entire nation, and ultimately builds a movement of churches to reach the world, must be like the man from La Mancha. That man dreamed an impossible dream. Is reaching the world and completing the Great Commission impossible? Whatever Jesus commanded us to do, He expected will be done, and He will supply His faith and power to fulfill His command.

Remember, a church is never a human invention, Jesus said, "I will build My church." Also, a church planting movement is never built by an isolated man, but will be built by a man of faith who completes the task in the power of Jesus Christ. Why? Because faith unleashes the spiritual power of Jesus. God uses average men, of extraordinary faith, to build or begin a movement. He uses leaders faced with insurmountable odds, usually possessing limited resources in unlikely circumstances, defying the odds and winning victory after victory over satan—not to mention the leader will have to deal with some of his own defeats and reversals—to build a church or movement that is ultimately a creation of God.

A church is people; the Greek word *ecclesia* means "out-called people." So, God calls a man from sin and the attractions of the world to follow Him, serve Him, and win lost people to Christ. He must master the message, move mountains by faith, and build a church by the power of God. In the process he does what average humans can't do—he builds a church or movement by faith for the glory of God.

When you see a church or movement of churches exploding on the scene and winning thousands to Christ, you know it was not built by a mere human, but by God. God anoints the leader's spiritual gifts, answers prayers, and honors faith to move mountains and defeat satan. It is the result of the Holy Spirit convicting people of sin, taking away their blindness, and presenting Christ to them.

Satan hates God and the children of God. Satan has never loved a church, nor will his followers support a church unless it is for their selfish purpose. The basic motivation of sinful people is self-gain and self-pleasure. They obey their nature, mimic the times, and refuse to obey God. Therefore, they hate church because it challenges their priorities, it condemns their sin, and refuses to condone their pleasures, addictions, sins, and corrupt living.

A soul-winning church will always convict the surrounding people by its purity, humility, and allegiance to Jesus Christ. The word *convict* means "to cause to see." As a result, they see their sin through God's eyes, and they are confronted with judgment waiting for them at death. The witch doctors have never supported the gospel-preaching preacher, nor have the human traffickers, harlots, liquor industry, gamblers, and all those who fight against God and His righteousness.

Into a dark world steps a man of faith anointed by God, called to leave everything and surrender to Jesus Christ. He gives up wealth, selfish glory, powerful positions, and goes to lost people, even to uncivilized tribes with the light of the gospel of Jesus Christ. He goes to blinded people who do not respect his knowledge, wisdom, or ecclesiastical stature. He simply says, "Here am I, Lord, send me" (see Isa. 6:8).

God always uses a man of faith. When the world was threatened by sexual and demonic abuse, one man of faith followed the God of heaven—Noah. When the nations were given over to idolatry, one man of faith believed in the God of creation—Abraham. When the world faced seven hideous years of famine and starvation, God gave one man of faith the solution—Joseph. When the people of God were inhumanly persecuted in Egyptian slavery, God's man of faith delivered them—Moses. God always uses a man of faith who steps into an impossible situation, who faces insurmountable challenges and terrifying consequences, yet a man of faith with limited resources anointed with God's power has always won a victory. His name was Joshua, Gideon, Samuel, David, Elijah, Daniel, Jeremiah, and Paul.

Also, we could call the name of a modern man who stepped into that situation—Brian Houston, David Mohan, Alex Abraham, David Sobrepeña, Enoch Adeboye, Chris Hodges, Suliasi Kurulo, and many others.

One of the greatest tasks a man can do on earth is start a church. Jesus said, "I will build My church," but He always used a servant to start a church. The church is more than a human organization; the Bible calls it a body, "the body of Christ" (Eph. 1:22). The church is Jesus, so a man of faith and Jesus go out to plant a church together. Nothing is greater in life than starting a church.

But what about starting a movement of churches? Isn't starting a movement of churches greater? No! There is nothing greater than planting the first church because that church is Jesus Christ…it is His body on earth. When you see a church movement spread out across the land, you see Jesus in many places reaching lost people with salvation. No, a movement of churches is not the greatest. It would not have existence if there was not that first church. The first church is the greatest, a miracle, a work of God. So where does that leave the movement of churches? They are the product of one church that has become many churches, many miracles, many God-called men of faith.

Chris Hodges has a vision of planting a church in every large grouping of people in Alabama. Is that greater than planting one church? No! Hodges had originally planted the Church of the Highlands in Birmingham, Alabama, and his faith told him what could happen through the church. So, he has a vision of planting multi-sites all over the state. Therefore, a movement of churches is not more important than the first church; it is simply the fruit of a vision of completing the Great Commission. Yes, a movement of churches is dedicated to its unique doctrine and orderly organization to expedite its ministry. It may be bigger, but that doesn't mean it is better or superior. Greater than a movement of churches is the first church from which they all came.

Do you think God was pleased when He created Adam and Eve—the prototype of all that were to follow? Yes! Thereafter, Adam is referred to as "the first Adam." So Cain and Abel were not greater than their father, Adam. Nor was Noah greater than Adam who began it all.

So, beginning an original church is better than beginning a movement. Why? Because the life in the first church is extended into all the churches that follow. The first light and life extend to all new believers in all the new churches that follow.

Think of Martin Luther and the great movement he began for God. He not only introduced reformation to Christianity, he inspired a multitude of "Lutherans" who reproduced his original Lutheran church. Yet, he is known today as the father of Germany. When he translated the Bible into one German dialect out of all German dialects (there were approximately 15 German tribes and dialects in his day), he unified the German language into one language. Today, there are multiple Lutheran churches and there are multiple Lutheran denominations.

Think of John Wesley beginning the Methodist church in England. He began planting churches all over England, in every place his horse would carry him, and in every location where he preached. Then churches were planted every place Wesley's disciples preached. Ultimately, his circuit riders planted Methodist churches across England, the United States, and the world. While the United Methodist Church of the United States is one of the larger denominations in the world, there are multiple denominations of Methodists in the U.S. and around the world.

It's notable that those who planted churches and founded ministries of churches in this book did not have great university educations, nor did their churches spring from the ivy halls of academia, nor did they come from other established denominations. No! These men of faith who founded movements of churches were church planters who began planting one church, with their faith and vision. Their ministry extended to a church movement attempting to reach lost people for Jesus Christ.

Look again in Scripture, "God chose things the world considers foolish in order to shame those who think they are wise. And he chose things that are powerless to shame those who are powerful. God chose things despised by the world, things counted as nothing at all, and used them to bring to nothing what the world considers important. As a result, no one can ever boast in the presence of God" (1 Cor. 1:27-29 NLT).

There is a vast potential in a man when he is spirit-filled, dedicated, prays for miracles, exercises his faith to move mountains, and attempts to win as many lost people to Jesus Christ as possible.

To build a great church—or a great movement of churches—a leader must develop a hard-headed tenacity, "I'll never give up." He must also nurture a spiritual meekness to say, "Not I, but Christ." He begins with faith, prayer, study, and working sixty hours a week with the emotional strength to not crack when young converts deny the faith. He must have a reverent sense of the spiritual as he deals with unsaved people, but at the same time he must have the cold, calculating eye of a businessman who must balance a budget and use money for the glory of God. He must be quick to acquire knowledge in a thousand areas where he is ignorant, and at the same time he must lead authoritatively, knowing where he is going when no one else knows how to build a church, how to grow a church, or how to reach the world for Christ.

He must speak persuasively in sermons, yet listen sympathetically to personal problems of the lowest of his members. He must be extraordinarily equipped with spiritual gifts, an iron will, smarter than the Ph.D., more far-sighted than a millionaire who has accumulated wealth, and wiser than a corporate mogul who leads an organization of hundreds, thousands, and millions. He is not overwhelmed with billions!

If he doesn't have all this when he begins, he must learn it all as he grows. He may acquire experience, all in the process of building a growing, expanding church or church ministry to the glory of God.

While he is growing in faith, his organizational vision must expand, as well as acquiring skills for the movement that he is directing.

> ➤ As Daniel stood before lions...
> ➤ As David stood before Goliath...
> ➤ As Elijah stood alone on Mt. Carmel...

Tomorrow, future young men will go out as these ministry builders have done, because the work of God is not yet finished.

Only God can accentuate a man's talent, while at the same time compensate for his weaknesses. God uses the inadequate individual with meager abilities and marginal equipment to minister in difficult circumstances to build a church. It's a massive vision God has given to him to build one church then grow to a vision for many churches.

This vision is fueled by knowledge that people are going to hell; he knows only compassionate love can get them saved. Only a fearful knowledge that judgement day is coming will motivate a man of faith to surrender everything to God. It is also fueled by gratitude that God has saved him by the blood of Christ. That innate knowledge will motivate a man of faith to plant one church, then with an expanding vision plant more churches, all in the same obedience to the Great Commission so that his life's ministry reflects gratitude to Christ's power.

When a man is obedient to God's calling, and filled with the Holy Spirit, and anointed for ministry, and is single minded in reaching the world for Jesus Christ—then he can plant one church and then multiply his efforts by planting more churches. These churches together can then cooperate to complete the Great Commission.

Never has the power of God been more demonstrated in church planting and church multiplication than is evidenced in these new church planting movements. The men of faith who plant churches are pioneers, possessing traits only a few have. Men who build church movements must be like the founding fathers of a nation who pull together a vast multitude of people from a vast number of places within the culture to accomplish together what they couldn't separately.

When a man says yes to the call of God, he must find power in the presence of Christ. Then the man of faith must master the Bible that encompasses his life. Next, he must learn to build sermons to communicate God's message to the hearts and heads of listeners, counsel the hurting, rebuke the sinning, teach the ignorant—and do it all quickly, abundantly, and successfully. He usually begins with little, if with anything at all. He must lead people to Christ, nurture them in the Scriptures, train them in service, and aspire them to spiritual greatness.

The leader of faith must not bounce from one project to another, but rather have a rugged determination to "plant" and also patience to "water" (1 Cor. 3:6).

The church planter is like the self-made businessman who can do it all, because all depends upon him. He must be clothed in rugged individualism yet inwardly yielded to God who does it all through him. However, with time his role changes and his self-perception of new tasks and new responsibilities grows. As others with the gift of leadership arise in the church, his role as pastor-planter changes. He then must share his ministry with deacons or church boards who first help him supervise the church, then they do ministry without him as he moves on to bigger and more challenging roles. He must minister through those who manage ministry, and he must teach through Sunday school teachers, and preach through those who fill the many pulpits he's created.

THE ENDING FUTURE

The man of faith must build an organization for ministry, and within time that organization will minister to him. When he plants a church, he plants his faith, including his vision, his anointing, his loyalty to the Bible, his doctrine, and his view of worship and ministry. As he grows a church, it grows with him in spirituality. In time the church grows him in expanded ministry.

Along with that, he is building up his co-workers and co-intercessors. In the early days of church planting his faith is indispensable, but with time, his faith joins with the faith of many others who build with him the church of Jesus Christ. Ultimately building a movement of churches is creating a task force of congregations to carry out the Great Commission. Now what happens? The authority the church planter gives up to others in the church to grow the church comes back to him, as he now has a greater authority to lead a greater work for God—a movement of churches. Like a giant naval armada of ships can accomplish what a single ship cannot, so a movement of churches can do much more than any one church can do alone.

Appendix B

BIBLIOGRAPHY:

Ten of the Largest Church Ministries
Touching the World

CHAPTER ONE:

The Church of the Highlands—
Birmingham, Alabama—Chris Hodges

About Us: Association of Related Churches, ARChurches.com,
Chris Hodges (bio, age, family, etc.) informationcrodle.com

Church of the Highlands, Wikipedia

"Church of the Highland Is the Largest Congregation in Alabama,"
Greg Garrisons, USA Today, February 19, 2011

"Pastor of Fastest Growing U.S. Church Empowers Volunteers,"
Ronald Keener, Church Central, June 9, 2009

What's Next, Chris Hodges, Thomas Nelson Publishers, 2019, 250
pages (New York Times, bestseller's list)

CHAPTER TWO:

Hillsong—Sydney, Australia—Brian Houston

Brian Houston, Wikipedia

"Brian Houston Calls Hillsong a Contemporary Church: Not Classic Pentecostal," by Christy Gibson, *The Christian Post*, June 23, 2018

"Hillsong: A Church with Rock Concerts and 2 Million Followers," August 13, 2019, bbc.com

Hillsong Church, Wikipedia

"Hillsong Threatens Australia Media Over Brian Houston," C. Kelly, reporter coverage, September 26, 2018, the newdaily.com

"How Hillsong and Other Pentecostal Megachurches Are Refining Religion in Australia," by Stephen Stockwell and Ruby Jones, abc.net.au

"Inside the Hillsong Church's Money-Making Machine, by Deborah Snow," *The Sydney Morning Herald*, November 13, 2015

"Latest News on The Hillsong Church," *The Guardian*, theguardian.com

Live Love Lead: Your Best Is Yet to Come, by Brian Houston, Hachette Book Group, France (third largest publishing company in the world), 2015

"Megachurch with a Beat Lures a Young Flock," *The New York Times*, September 9, 2014.

CHAPTER THREE:

Life.Church—Edmond, Oklahoma—Craig Groeschel

Bobby Gruenewald, "My Entrepreneurial and Faith Journey," ELO Network, entrepreneurialendies.com

Bobby Gruenewald, Outreach Magazine, read articles by Bobby in this monthly Christian magazine

Bobby Gruenewald, Wikipedia

Craig Groeschel, "Alcheton: The Free Social Encyclopedia," August 29, 2018

Craig Groeschel, Wikipedia

Craig Groeschel, Wikiquote

How Churches and Leaders Can Get It and Keep It, by Craig Groeschel, Zondervan, August 2008

Life.Church, Wikipedia

"Oklahoma's Life.Church Founder Says He Is Never One to Play It Safe," by Cara Hinton, the Oklahoma, April 8, 2018

Twenty-five Largest Churches in America, by Sarah Burns, October 11, 2017

YouVersion, Wikipedia

"Virtual Vitality: Bobby Gruenewald Likes Technology and the Church," by Chris Norton, Christianity Today, November 19, 2011

CHAPTER FOUR:

World Harvest Center—Suva, Fiji—Suliasi Kurulo

From the Ends of the Earth, by Suliasi Kurulo, published by CMFI Publishers (Christian Mission Fellowship International), 2014, 200 pages

Rev. Kurulo: Man on a Mission, Fiji Sun, by Nemani Delaibatiki, September 28, 2019

Suliasi Kurulo, Wikipedia

"Ten Global Churches Larger Than American Churches," by James O. Davis, Church Leadership, January 16, 2016

World Harvest Radio, Wikipedia

CHAPTER FIVE:

The Redeemed Christian Church of God— Nigeria, Africa—Enoch Adeboye

"A Correlational Study of Servant Leadership and Successful Church Planting: A Case Study of The Redeemed Christian Church of God," Ph.D. dissertation, by James Oladipo Fadele, 2012

"A New Paradigm of Pentecostal Powers: A Study of the Redeemed Christian Church of God," JoKwabena Asamoah-Gyade, Cambridge University Press, April 2010

"Adeboye's Story: From Lecture Hall to Blended Pulpit," preaching. com, Nigeria, January 8, 2017

Days of Destiny, E.A. Adeboye, Technopol Publishers, Ibadan, Nairobi, 2012, 496 pages

Enoch Adeboye, Wikipedia

"Gospel Resounds in African Tongues," by David Watkins, New York Times, April 18, 2014. (Claims there are 14 parishes in New York area in 2004)

"Mentoring as a Tool for Leadership Development in The Redeemed Christian Church of God," by Babatunde Oladimeji, D.Min. dissertation, Asbury Theological Seminary, Asbury, Kentucky

"Mission from Africa," by Andrew Rice, New York Times, November 19, 2011

"Political Spiritualization: Pentecostal Revival in Nigeria," Ruth Marshall, University of Chicago Press, 2009, page 74

"The Pentecostal Revolution in Nigeria," Musa A. B. Gaiya, Occosional Paper, Center of African Studies, University of Copenhagen

"Revenge Mission and the Establishment of the Redeemed Christian Church in Canada," by DaleJemirado, Missionala, ISBN 2312-67BX, volume 45, number 3, Pretoria, Africa

"The Challenges of Missionary Training in the 21st Century," MA Thesis, Liberty University, USA, by Kola Alyedogbon

The Redeemed Church of God, Wikipedia

"The Redeemed Christian Church of God, Nigeria, Local Identities and Global Processes in African Pentecostalism," Ph.D. dissertation by Asonzeh Franklin-Kennedy, University Bayreuth, epub. uni-bayreuth.de

"The Redeemed Christian Church of God," by Babtunde Oladimeji, Ph.D. Asbury, Theological Seminary Asbury, Kentucky

"Trademark of Humility, Pastor Enoch Adeboye," by Christine Chisha Daily-Mail.co.zim, Zambia, November 2014

CHAPTER SIX:

Global Church Network—
Orlando, Florida—James O. Davis

Beyond All Limits: The Synergistic Church for a Planet in Crisis, by Bill Bright and James O. Davis, Google books, Amazon.com

Billion Soul Harvest, Wikipedia

Global Church Network, Facebook.com

Guttenberg to Google: The 20 Indispensable Laws of Commitment, by James O. Davis, published by Billion Soul Harvest

Synergize, www.synergize. TV/sponsor/billion-soul-network

The Billion Soul Story, by James O. Davis, published by Billion Soul Harvest, 2013

The Global Church Learning Center, www.globalchurchlearning-center.com

We Are the Church: The Untold Story of God's Global Awakening, by James O. Davis and Leonard Sweet, published by Billion Soul Harvest, 2016

CHAPTER SEVEN:

Glory of Zion—Denton, Texas—Chuck Pierce

Apostolic Church Arising: God's People Gathering and Contending, by Chuck D. Pierce and Robert Heidler, published by Glory of Zion Ministry, PO Box 1601, Denton, Texas, 2015, 196 pages

Experiencing the Spirit, by Robert Heidler, Chosen, Baker Publishing Group, Minneapolis, Minnesota, 1998, 260 pages

Glory of Zion: America Whirling Dervish of a Service, by Christy Thomas, *The Thoughtful Pastor, Newsletter,* (This is a sarcastic description of a worship service). Patheogy.com

God Is Raising a Gideon's Army, January 2016, https://ufnk6.com.

The Messianic Church Arising, by Robert D. Heidler, published by Glory of Zion Ministry, 224 pages

"We Are in 21 Days of Divine Access," by Chuck Pierce, *Charisma Magazine,* December 5, 2016

CHAPTER EIGHT:

New Life Assembly of God— Chennai, India—David Mohan

A 40 Year Jubilee: New Life Assembly of God Church, 1973-2013, by David E. Stewart Sr., 106 pages, published independently

"Asian Leaders Honored," *Assembly of God News,* June 2, 2017

"Christian Leaders Gathering in Chennai to Dedicate the Largest Assembly of God Church," published in *Christian Today,* Ecumenical Press, by Surojit Chatterjee, May 8, 2004

Impact on India, Billy Graham Evangelistic Association, by Janet Chrisman, February 1, 2010

India: Learning from New Life, Outreach Magazine, by Warren Bird, January 6, 2016

New Life Assembly of God, Wikipedia, http://wikipedia.org

New Life Assembly of God Church Built Through Faith, by David Mohan, booklet, 16 pages, published by the church

New Life Growth Stories, by David Mohan, booklet, 50 pages, published by church.

Ten Global Churches Larger Than America's Largest, by James O. Davis, Church Leaders, 2019

The Madras Miracle, by David Mohan, with David Grant, published by Assemblies of God World Mission, Springfield, Missouri, 2005

What We Can Learn from Large Growing Churches Overseas, Leadership Network, by Warren Bird, August 15, 2018

CHAPTER NINE:

Word of Hope—Manila, Philippines—David Sobrepeña

Church Online, gotochruchonline.tv

David Sobrepeña, davidsobrepena.com

"Dr. David Sobrepeña: Founder Word of Hope Christian Church," Filipino Christian Achievers, Christpinoy.blogspot.com

Pentecostal Mega Churches in Southeast Asia, by Terence Dona Publisher, Iseas-Yusof Ishak Institute, 2019

Rev. David Sobrepeña, Wikimedia

Spirit Wind International, spiritwind.org

Ten Global Churches Larger than America's Largest, by James O. Davis, published by Billion Soul Harvest, Orlando, Florida, 2012

"Word of Hope Christian Family Celebrates its 26th Anniversary," www.pagc.ag.news

CHAPTER TEN:

Dr. Raj—South Asia

No biographical material listed by request of Dr. Raj because of
persecution of this church ministry in South Asia.

Appendix C

DEFINITIONS AND DESCRIPTIONS
of Faith Terms and Words

FAITH:
BIBLE DEFINITION (HEBREWS 11:1)

> "Faith is the substance of things hoped for, the evidence of things not seen" (NKJV).

> "[Faith] is the confident assurance that something we want is going to happen. It is the certainty that what we hope for is waiting for us, even though we cannot see it up ahead" (TLB).

> "Only faith can guarantee the blessings that we hope for, or prove the existence of realities that are unseen" (NJB).

> "Faith makes us sure of what we hope for and gives us proof of what we cannot see" (CEV).

Administration Faith: using the ability and desire God has given to put the right people in the right place, at the right time, to do the right task, with the right tools and ability to the glory of God.

Administrative Faith: is using the spiritual gift of organizing things, events and people in the right place at the right time, for the right reason, for the spiritual ministry and growth of both people and the work of Christ.

Circle of Faith Ministry: when more than one person exercises their outward expression of faith to a believer about a problem or a situation or event affecting the group; a circle of faith by all will cause the growth of faith in one member or many.

Discipling Faith: is fulfilling the command of Jesus Christ to do all the tasks that are necessary to move another believer, usually a new believer, toward full maturity.

Evangelism Faith: begins with a burden for a lost person/all people, a desire to share the Good News of the gospel with them, explaining that they are sinners who are lost and will be punished by God after death for their sins, how Jesus Christ paid their debt of sin and has forgiven them by His substitutionary death, and asking the person to receive Christ as Savior and become a child of God.

Exhortation Faith: is the ability to use your example, biblical knowledge, Christian maturity to motivate another believer to fulfill a task or responsibly.

Faith Applied Correctly: faith must correctly interpret the principles of Scripture and properly apply them to the problem or crises it faces.

Faith Converging with One's Spiritual Gift: leaders will speak faith more effectively to a problem and/or crisis when the issue is related to their spiritual giftedness.

Faith Praying: obeying Jesus' command to ask God to give the answer you seek because you believe He promised to do it (Mark 11:24), because you abide in Him (John 15:7), because you ask according to Scriptures (1 John 3:22), because you ask according to the will of God (1 John 5:14), because you ask continually (Matthew 7:7), because you know He will answer (John 16:23-24).

Faith Worship: a total intellectual, emotional, and volitional response of praise, exaltation, and gratitude to God based on a regeneration experience, prompted by the Holy Spirit, resulting into exaltation of God's glory.

Giving Faith: is exercising the spiritual gift of giving one's self to another and/or for the cause of Christ that includes sacrificing/donating time, talent, and treasure.

Gratitude Faith: is the positive response of the heart for the good things enjoyed in life, as well as disappointing and dangerous things in life knowing "all things work together for good to those who love God and are called according to His purpose" (Rom. 8:28).

Helping Faith: is exercising the spiritual gift of showing kindness by assistance, working with, or doing the task for another.

Intercession Faith: our belief in God gives us access to God in prayer so that when we pray confidently for an answer, God sends an answer.

Introspective Faith: because of our faith in God, He shows us truth about ourself as we come to Him in prayer for answers.

Intimate Faith with God: seeking and receiving the presence of God in your life as you approach Him and abide in Jesus and He abides in you (John 14:20).

Life-Giving Faith Principles: the Bible has the life of both the incarnate Jesus, the Word of God (John 1:1,14), and the written Word of God also called the Word of faith (Romans 10:8); when you exercise faith based on the spoken or written Word of God it will lead to supernatural results when applied to problems or a crisis.

Meditation Faith: your faith will grow as you think about and meditate on the Word of God. It is based on listening to Scripture, reading, studying, and memorizing the Bible.

Mercy-Showing Faith: using the spiritual gift of empathy and sympathy to encourage and sustain another person in and through situations that are difficult.

Prayer Healing Faith: the ability to effectively intercede to God for healing of the sick according to the direction of James 5:13-16.

Praise Faith: is glorifying and exalting God for His divine nature and attributes, for all He has done for your salvation in the death and resurrection of Christ, and for all He does for you in your life.

Prevailing Faith: because an issue and ministry is biblical in nature and God has led in exercising faith for that issue or ministry, one must continue believing God for the answer or solution of the problem/issue at hand, as well as continuing in ministry or working toward a satisfactory end.

Prioritizing Faith: because all ministries are equal when measured by faith and truth, yet all things must be prioritized to meet the needs/crisis of the situation at hand; leaders must understand and apply the principles of faith because of the priority of time, effort, and resources.

Rebuilding Faith: is sharing with another the biblical standard for right attitude, right belief, right living, and right serving, because they need direction and correction.

Shepherding Faith: is expressing a desire to give spiritual care and protection to another by praying for them, teaching them, counseling them; all the while being an example to them of a victorious Christian life.

Resting Faith: is being silent as you wait before God for the answer.

Repentance Faith: technically, we cannot turn from sin resulting in our new birth and regenerating, but as we turn to Jesus our Savior and trust in Him for salvation, we become new creatures in Jesus Christ (2 Cor. 5:17).

Searching Faith: when you know that God is leading you, but you don't know what to do or where to go, you continue to wait on God for the answer or guidance.

Soul-Winning Faith: the ability and desire to communicate the gospel in an understandable manner so a lost person

TEN *of the* LARGEST CHURCH MINISTRIES AGGRESSIVELY TOUCHING THE WORLD

responds to Jesus Christ in salvation and follows Him in obedience and service.

Spiritual Gift of Faith: when God gives spiritual abilities for you to serve Him, He also gives a serving gift of faith to us in ministry. Faithfulness in your gift of faith will grow your faith.

Spiritual Warfare Faith: is praying against the works of satan and his demons as we ask for victory over the world, the flesh, and the devil in our intercession.

Teaching Faith: is the spiritual gift to study, learn, and share with individuals or a group the biblical lessons for Christian growth, living, and serving.

Testifying Faith: is sharing with others how God saved you, usually including your life before salvation, how you were saved, and what Jesus Christ means to you now.

Thanksgiving Faith: is appreciation to God for the benefits enjoyed, lessons learned, and/or an improved situation.

Transforming Faith: you will be changed and renewed when you learn God's power and love for your life and all He has done for you.

Vision Faith: is seeing the potential in projects, events, and people that could be done by God for His work and glory, and applying the potential of what God can do in the situation by prayers, planning with an aim to act on the vision.

Vow of Faith: when you understand scriptural principles relating to an issue, you have examined it to understand the circumstances of an issue, and God is leading you to an answer/

solution, then you vow in faith to work for the answer and commit yourself to its fulfillment.

Worship Faith: is obeying the commands of Scripture to offer praise, adoration, and worship to God. It involves using the passage of worship to God found in the Bible in your prayers.

About

DR. ELMER L. TOWNS

Dr. Elmer L. Towns is Dean Emeritus of the School of Religion and Theological Seminary at Liberty University, which he cofounded in 1971. He continues to teach the Pastor's Bible Class at Thomas Road Baptist Church each Sunday, which is televised on a local network and Angel One.

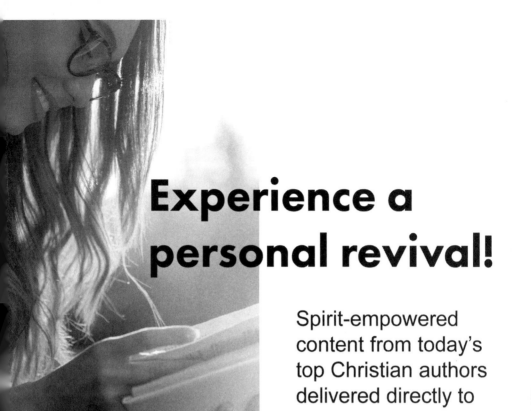